Make, Bake
 and Celebrate...
with
Polly & Jago
2008

Make, Bake and Celebrate...

with Polly & Jago
2008

Text by Sarah Rowden
Photography by Joanna Vestey
Illustration by Mark Beech
With a foreword by Kris Murrin

Acknowledgements – For Polly and Jago,
Chloe and Tom, Martin and Steve – and for
all our fabulous helpers along the way
– Bruce, Jessica, Mary, Alex, Carolina,
Lucy, Francis D, the team at Resolution
Creative, the team at St Helen's Foodstore
– and for our little models Georgie, Ben and
Tashie, Bona B, Clementine, Max and Amber,
Pirate Oscar and the many others who
contributed so much –
Thank you all xx Sarah and Jo.

Contents

Foreword

When I heard that one of London's best loved "foodies" and a world renowned photographer were joining forces to create a book, I was excited. Their end product does not disappoint. There are gorgeous photos and illustrations; recipes that are quick, easy and absolutely delicious. But what this delightful book delivers is so much more than the sum of its parts. It is a beautifully crafted and timely reminder of all that is important and central to our lives.

Three-quarters of families in the UK have parents who both work. This means that if your life is anything like mine it tends to whizz by in a hectic blur. We blink and the toddler we were taking to nursery is starting secondary school! This book shows us how to slow down and relish the passing seasons. It challenges us to take some time each month to celebrate the rituals and customs that bind a family together; to choose to create the memories we can cherish above all else.

Sarah and Jo deliver their message in such a charming and simple manner, I for one can find no excuse not to follow them!

Kris Murrin

Introduction

Throughout the year we Britons celebrate or mark lots of special days and festivals and remember certain people or occasions. Sometimes it may be a religious holiday celebrated by many, other times we may find just the excuse we need to stop juggling our busy daily lives and do something fun together.

These precious moments create gorgeous lasting memories, which we hope our children will cherish, passing them on to their children, and "carrying the torch" so to speak.

A lot of British celebrations have very little to do with race or faith but stem from ancient folklore often dating back as far as Viking, Roman or French invasions. In days gone by the calendar was dominated by the moon and stars, the four seasons and the cycle of both human and animal life.

We refer to many of the festivals from these times as Pagan. Pagan means unrelated to any god of any faith, but they celebrate the importance of Mother Nature and our earthly wonders. Many of these we still find on our calendar today: Harvest Festival, Summer Solstice, May Day and Yuletide are just a few that help us to understand our British history and underpin the role of tradition and ritual in our lives.

These celebrations are a chance for families and communities alike to draw together and strengthen the bonds between them. It's a chance to build upon our past traditions and perhaps set in motion new ones. We still do lots of thing our grandmothers did at Christmas and we have a Jewish friend who always makes the same cake for Passover that her mother, grandmother and great-grandmother had made.

Make, Bake and Celebrate brings together a huge array of historical facts, remarkable legends, delicious and simple recipes and exciting and easily achievable craft projects in one easy-to-use compendium. All our projects use basic, inexpensive, easy-to-source ingredients and equipment, most can be found in many of the major supermarkets, home ware stores or art and craft suppliers.

We have loved making the recipes and crafts here with our many helpers. We very much hope you enjoy them too and would love to hear about any things you have particularly enjoyed or would like to see featured in Make, Bake and Celebrate 2009 with Polly and Jago – Please visit www.pollyandjago.com to tell us more.

Happy making baking and celebrating!

Sarah and Jo

It's assumed an adult will be supervising all the cooking and craft projects. All recipes will serve four people unless stated. Some projects may become week-long endeavours where others are just there to fill a rainy afternoon – you will find these three symbols on each month's calendar. They will guide you through the activities on the following pages. Where you see a saucepan there will be a recipe, where you find a pair of scissors you will find a craft and when the symbol of the book is shown there will be an amazing or informative fact or legend, and unfold the cover to find a beautifully illustrated and informative wall calendar for 2008.

January

Auld Lang Syne

Should auld acquaintance be forgot,
And never brought to mind?
Should auld acquaintance be forgot,
And auld lang syne?

  For auld lang syne, my dear,
  for auld lang syne,
  we'll tak a cup o' kindness yet,
  for auld lang syne.

And surely ye'll be your pint-stoup!
And surely I'll be mine!
And we'll tak a cup o' kindness yet,
for auld lang syne.

We twa hae run about the braes,
and pou'd the gowans fine;
but we've wander'd mony a weary fit,
sin' auld lang syne.

We twa hae paidl'd in the burn,
frae morning sun till dine;
but seas between us braid hae roar'd
sin' auld lang syne.

And there's a hand, my trusty fiere!
And gies a hand o' thine!
And we'll tak a right gude-willie-
   waught,
for auld lang syne.

by Robert Burns 1759—1796

1st month

XI

January's flower is the Snowdrop   January's gemstone is the Garnet   January is named after the Roman god Janus

MON	TUES	WED	THURS	FRI	SAT	SUN
	New Year's Day Hogmanay Global Family Day **1**	**2**	Martin Luther King Day (USA) **3**	JRR Tolkien, author. Born 1892 **4**	12th Night Birthday Guru Gobind Singh (Sikh) Wassailing the apple tree **5**	Epiphany (3 wise men arrive to see Jesus) Joan of Arc, heroine of France. Born 1412 **6**
St Distaff's Day Feast of the Nativity (Orthodox Christian) Galileo discovered Jupiter 1610 **7**	**8**	**9**	Al-Hijra, Muslim New Year League of Nations. Established 1920 **10**	**11**	**12**	St Hilary's Day Make Your Dreams Come True Day One World Week **13**
Maghi (Sikh) **14**	**15**	**16**	Robert Scott reached south pole 1912 Wassailing the Orchards (Sussex) **17**	AA Milne, author of Winnie the Pooh Born 1882 **18**	Ashura (Islam) Paul Cezanne, painter. Born 1839 **19**	World Religion Day (Bahai) **20**
BBC made its 1st world broadcast in 1930 **21**	Mahayana New Year (Buddhist) Tu B'shvat (Jewish) **22**	**23**	Gold discovered in California 1848 Sir Winston Churchill, politician. Died 1965 **24**	Burns Night St Dwynwen's Day Patron Saint of lovers **25**	Australia Day Republic Day (India) **26**	Holocaust Memorial Day Mozart, composer. Born 1756 **27**
National Storytelling Week **28**	National Potato Day Galileo sighted Neptune 1613 **29**	**30**	Bug Busting Day **31**			

Capricorn 22nd December – 20th January

Aquarius 21st January – 19th February

Hi Jago

We have been really busy today taking down all the Christmas decorations to stop any bad luck for next year, got to be quick mum wants to wassail the apple tree later! I think my mum is a bit barmy she and some mates are going to sing songs to the apple trees to make them grow fruit bit chilly for me though.

lots of love Polly XX

Jago Harris

204 Latimer Road

London W10 6QY

Hi Polly

Hope you are well — do you fancy coming over to mine for a mad hatter's tea party? You could be Alice and I can be mad as a hatter Te he he do you think your mum be the queen of hearts and bring some jammie tarts?

from Jago

Polly Loughney

Honeysuckle Cottage

Lower Baldridge
Oxon OX8 4PT

Potato Family

Other Ideas

1. Choose your potatoes. We like to use wobbly-shaped spuds, which gives their faces more character.

2. Give them a wash and decide which way is up and which way is down.

3. Take a little slice off the bottom so that he or she can stand up. Then decide what he or she is going to look like.

4. Either copy our accessories or make your own and stick them on to card. Colour them in or decorate them with glitter. Then cut the shapes out.

5. We think it's easier to glue these on, but you can use dress pins to pin them on if you prefer. The quicker and easier, the better!

What about?

You could make these potato heads into skittles. Award points for each head and keep score for how many you knock down by rolling a tennis ball at them.

What about making a stamp for printing with the bottom of your spud. Cut a shape out, dip it in paint and hop your potato across some paper or even a t-shirt.

You will need

Potatoes, scissors, paper or card, glitter, crayons, pens, glue, dress pins.

Magic Mash Mountain

What to do

Peel the potatoes and boil them until soft.
Then drain them and add the milk and butter,
and mash them all up until smooth. Sometimes
we add cheese or parsley to our potatoes, but
there are all sorts of other flavours you can
add like mustard or onions. Add the salt and
pepper until they taste just the way you like.
Meanwhile put a pan of water on to boil.
When it's bubbling away add the purple
sprouting broccoli until that's soft, use tongs
to lift it out of the water and leave it to one
side. Swirl the same boiling water around
the pan with a spoon and crack the eggs into
the middle of the whirlpool. We like our eggs
runny so we let them simmer in the water
for 4 minutes (but you can cook them longer)
and then lift them out with a draining spoon
and sit them on a bit of kitchen roll while
you start to plate up. First put a good dollop
of mash in the middle of 4 plates and make
a little dip in the top to rest the egg on.
Then stand the broccoli up in the
bottom of the mash and it's ready
to eat. The best bit is popping
the egg and letting the yolk
run out.

Ingredients

4 large potatoes good for mashing
(we used **King Edwards**)
40g butter
salt and pepper to taste
100ml milk
4 large eggs
purple sprouting broccoli

We made this on National Potato Day
really yummy!

Abracadabra triangle for unexpected good fortune!

```
              a
            a b
          a b r
Abracadabra  a b r a
triangle for  a b r a c
unexpected   a b r a c a
good        a b r a c a d
fortune!   a b r a c a d a
          a b r a c a d a b
         a b r a c a d a b r
        a b r a c a d a b r a
```

Did you know, potatoes are a great source of vitamin C. if you make chips with them they retain the most vitamin C of all potato dishes.

17

Solar System Mobile

You will need

Cardboard, string or thread, glue, card, paper, scissors, crayons and pens.

Begin by drawing a disc, marking all the points where the planets will be suspended. You can do this directly on to card or stick the cut-out disc on to a stiff piece of card. Paint or decorate it so that it looks like the night sky. We like sticking stars and glitter on it so that it looks like an extension of the galaxy.

Push the tip of a pen through the cardboard at all the points the planets are charted. Don't make the holes too big!

Draw or photocopy the planets, and stick them on to card as well. If you like you can colour them to look exactly like the photos we have all seen of the real thing. Alternatively, you could be a bit more abstract and use paints and crayons to decorate them in whatever style you want.

Make pen holes in the top of each planet and thread the pieces of string or twine through. Tie a knot the other side, so that the planet cannot slip off.

Push the other end of the planets' strings through the holes in the large top disc. Remember to match the right planet to the correct hole. Tie a knot at the top and do same for all the other planets.

Lift the top disc up and carefully arrange all the planets so that they dangle nicely around the moon. Finally, suspend your mobile. If you have made a really big mobile, it's best to tie it up from three points around the edge.

* These planets are not to scale

The Sun Venus Mercury Earth Mars Jupiter Uranus Saturn Neptune Pluto

Why don't you?

Use this to give you a rough guide of where each of the planets sits within our solar system, it's not exact, but it will give you the idea.

Radiant Rainbow Cupcakes

What to do

Pre-heat the oven to gas mark 6 or 200°C.
Blitz the sugar and butter together until they are soft and light in colour.
Add the eggs and beat them in, and then add the flour and vanilla.
Once all of these ingredients are mixed well together, add a little
of the milk at a time to make it a dropping consistency off the mixing
spoon. Next, spoon the mixture into paper cases in a muffin tray as
evenly as you can and then pop the tray in the oven. The cakes will
take about 15 minutes to cook, but watch them. They may take less
until they are golden brown and firm to the touch.

Once the cakes are out and cooling you can begin to make the icing.
Mix the sugar with a little water and then divide into 7 cups. Then
you can begin mixing in the colours of the rainbow. As soon as the
cakes are cooled, spoon on the icings and let them run out to the
edge of the paper case. It's a good idea to let the icing set before
you decorate the cakes with glitter. (We found our glitter from
edible art 01388 816309.)

The next thing is to eat them!

Ingredients

- 125g softened unsalted butter
- 125g caster sugar
- 2 large eggs
- 125g self-raising flour
- 1 teaspoon of vanilla extract
- 2-3 tablespoons of milk
- 500g royal icing sugar
- food colourings
- 12 muffin paper cases
- edible glitter
- 12 hole muffin tray

Cheer up cakes for January

You should eat a plateful of rainbow colours every day – that's what scientists say.

Try using a useful mnemonic to remember the order of the colours of the rainbow – Richard of York gave battle in vain.

January
Facts & Legends

New Year's Eve is celebrated all over the world. In England we wait for the bells of Big Ben to chime and party with lively fireworks, dancing and linking our arms together to sing "Auld Lang Syne" to remind ourselves of past, present and future friends.

Hogmanay

It's thought that Hogmanay celebrations were originally brought to Scotland in the 8th century by marauding, invading Vikings.

The Scots eat haggis, and drink whiskey maybe to keep out the cold, and they sing Auld Land Syne.

Burns Night
Robert Burns, born 25th of January 1759, was a famous Scottish poet, admired for his beautiful verse, love songs, funny humour, drinking and womanising. He wrote a special poem about the blessing of a haggis, which is read out at Hogmanay festivities.

Twelfth Night
On the 6th of January, originally the last day of Christmas, when all the decorations should be taken down to avoid bad luck for the following year.

1st of January

In medieval times, January 1st was very significant for superstitions and prosperity for the year ahead. It was tradition to put a flat cake on the horn of a cow in every farmyard. The farmers and their workers used to sing and dance around the cow until the cake fell to the ground. If it fell in front of the cow it signified good luck and if it fell behind, it was very bad.

On old Roman calendars, there was no January or February. New Year was in March for Romans, even when they added Januarius, and it only changed to January as the 1st month 250 years ago.

St Agnes' Eve

This was a day on which girls who wanted to marry soon would perform certain rituals before going to bed so they could dream of their future husbands. Some of the rituals included walking backwards upstairs to bed, saying the lord's prayer and taking one pin at a time from a pin cushion and transferring it to their sleeve, fasting all day, or eating a piece of dumb cake, made with friends in total silence, with a lot of salt in it too! Sweet dreams girls!

St Hilary's Feast Day

The 13th of January has gained the reputation of being the coldest day of the year. This probably dates back to 1086 when an Arctic freeze spread over the country and lasted until March. Even into the 15th, 16th, and 17th century the frosts were really sharp and long.

There was a famous frost fair in 1608 on the River Thames where bowling, tents, sideshows and food stalls were all set up.

February

Groundhog Day

In traditional weather lore, if a groundhog emerges from its burrow on this day and fails to see its shadow because the weather is cloudy, winter will soon end. If the groundhog sees its shadow because the weather is bright and clear, it will be frightened and run back into its hole, and the winter will continue for six more weeks.

2nd month

XII

February's flower is the Primrose | February's gemstone is the Amethyst | February has Valentine's Day. The god of love is Cupid

MON	TUES	WED	THURS	FRI	SAT	SUN
					Saraswati Day (Hindu) / Groundhog Day / Candlemas Day **2**	The Feast of St Blaize / First soft landing on the moon 1966 (Lunar 9 USSR) **3**
Halfway point of winter **4**	Shrove Tuesday (Christian) **5**	Ash Wednesday Lent begins (Christian) / Queen Elizabeth II came to the throne 1952 **6**	Start of Chinese New Year / Charles Dickens, author. Born 1812 **7**	Parinirvana Day (Buddhist) / Kissing Friday Jules Verne, author. Born 1828 **8**	**9**	**10**
Thomas Edison, inventor. Born 1847 **11**	Charles Darwin, naturalist. Born 1809 **12**	Blessing of the salmon nets (Northumberland) **13**	St Valentine's Day **14**	Britain went decimal 1971 / Galileo Galilei, scientist. Born 1564 **15**	**16**	Random Acts of Kindness Day **17**
18	**19**	The 1st cinema in Britain opened in 1896 **20**	**21**	World Thinking Day **22**	National Doodle Day / Dolly the sheep cloned 1997 / G F Handel, composer. Born 1685 **23**	**24**
25	**26**	Polar Bear Day **27**	**28**	Leap Year Day **29**		

Aquarius 21st January – 19th February

Pisces 20th February – 20th March

Hi Jago

Guess what? Today at my Hindu friend Indira's house everyone was wearing yellow! They were celebrating the first day of spring (the yellow stands for the warmth of spring). She told me about Saraswati, the goddess of music, poetry, dance and drama so we did lots of it.

big kiss Polly XX

Jago Harris

204 Latimer Road

London W10 6QY

Hi Polly

Kissing girls everywhere - yuk Apparently until the 1940's boys were allowed to kiss the girls on kissing Friday. If the girl said no you were allowed to pinch them on the bottom - much better than having to kiss them. Did you get any kisses or pinches?

See you soon Jago

Polly Loughney

Honeysuckle Cottage

Lower Baldridge
Oxon OX8 4PT

Chinese Lanterns

Other Ideas

You could use a hole punch to create a dotted effect on the lantern

*

How about attaching streamers to add extra impact to the lanterns?

*

You might like to try interweaving the lanterns with fairy lights. It'll add a festive sparkle whatever the occasion!

1 Fold the paper or card in half, lengthways.

2 Snip along the crease, up towards the outer edges, but don't go all the way, stop about 2 inches from the edge.

3 Unfold the paper and bend it around to stick the two shorter ends together with sticky tape.

4 Make a handle for the lantern by cutting a strip of card about 2cm wide and 15cm long. Then stick it from one side to the other, inside the lantern.

5 Go crazy with your decorations. Smother the lantern with glue and stick as much or as little to it as you like.

6 Hang your lanterns where light will catch it, so that it sparkles and shines.

You will need

Thick coloured paper or card (A4 or A5), glue, sticky tape, scissors, glitter, other pretty decorations.

Sweet Heart Valentine's Cookies

What to do

Get the oven hot to gas mark 4 or 180°C.
Cream the butter and sugar together until pale and then beat in the eggs and vanilla. On top of this, sift the flour, baking powder and salt and start to mix everything together. You can use a spoon or your hands but start slowly so you don't get flour everywhere. Once this comes together in a dough, take it out of the bowl, and gently knead it on a floured surface to make it smooth and pop it in the fridge for about an hour. When it's had a rest you can get it out of the fridge and roll it out on a floury surface until it's about half a centimetre thick. Cut into shapes with your cookie cutters and put them on to the tray and then into the oven. Bake them for about 8 – 12 minutes or until they are golden. Cool them on a rack and start to make your icing. Look at the pictures of how we iced them.

Ingredients

175g soft unsalted butter
200g caster sugar
2 large eggs
1 teaspoon of vanilla extract
400g plain flour
1 teaspoon of baking powder
1 teaspoon of salt
300g royal icing sugar
food colouring
cookie cutters
greased baking tray
1 piping bag

Jago made these for Polly - sweet!

Did you know cookies are slow-burning energy givers - in ancient times they were the original fast food.

The dough could be made with all sorts of delicious things - chocolate chips, oats, cherries, coconut are just a few of our favourites.

Valentine Cards

There are all sorts of beautiful designs that can be made into a Valentine card. Here are some ideas. For the one we really love, it is a simple card made with splishy splatter paper.

You will need

Paper, card, scissors, pens, paints, crayons, sticky tape, glue, plate and salad spinner.

Take your salad spinner, remove its basket for a minute while you cut the paper ready to position inside the bowl. You need to curl the paper around the inside edge of the bowl, making sure the surface of the paper is smooth against the sides.

Put the basket back in and put a plate in the bottom.

On to the plate, squirt your paints (poster paint is best). Make sure they are a bit runny, otherwise the paint won't splatter. Three colours are really enough.

Put the lid on and begin working the spinner. Turn it for about 20 seconds and then slow it down. What should happen is the paint flies off the plate on to the paper.

Take off the lid and carefully take out the basket, then the paper.

Leave the splattered paper for a day to ensure it is dry before using it.

Did you know?

Britain has its own Mrs Valentine. Every year Ann Noble, who runs the Post Office at Lover, Wiltshire, gets over 2,000 cards from people wanting the Lover postmark on their Valentine's Day cards. Try it by sending your card to: Ann Noble, Lover Post Office, Brown Bonnet, Besome Drove, Lover, Salisbury SP5 2PN.

♥ ♥

Did you know that in Victorian times it was thought bad luck to sign a Valentines Day card – there are lots of ways to disguise your signature so your valentine doesn't know its from you – you could try – cutting letters out of newspaper print and sticking into words, using your left hand – if you are very ambitious you could try writing with your feet, putting the pen between your toes – or you could just ask someone else to write it for you!

♥ ♥

There are lots of gifts of love people give to each other but perhaps the most amazing one was the Taj Mahal at Agra in India. Mughal Emperor Shah Jahan had it built in memory of his beautiful wife, Mumtaz Mahal. It was started in 1634 and took nearly 22 years. Around 20,000 workers from all over India and Central Asia were used.

♥ ♥

Here are some meanings of flowers which might be useful if you are thinking of sending flowers – Red Rose – Passionate love, Camellia – You are perfect in every way, Red Carnation – My heart aches for you, Daffodils – You're the only one for me, Blue Hyacinths – Our love is constant, Sunflower – I adore you, Red Tulip – You're a perfect lover, and one to avoid…Yellow Carnations – You disappoint me!

Polly's Perfect Pancakes

Ingredients

100g plain flour
a pinch of salt
1 large egg
250ml milk
butter to fry

What to do

Sieve the flour into a bowl. Make a well in the middle and crack in the egg and add ½ of the milk. Use a balloon whisk and begin drawing in the flour from the edge until you have a very thick batter. Whisk the batter until lots of bubbles appear on the top and then add the pinch of salt and the rest of the milk. Leave the batter alone for about ½ an hour and then get your frying pan at the ready. Melt a little butter in the pan and then pour in some of the batter and move the pan around to spread the mixture over the base. Leave it to brown underneath, then loosen it around the edges with a knife and try your best to flip the pancake and catch it in the pan. In our house we love lemon and sugar on pancakes but there are all sorts of toppings.
Look at the others we like.

There is an art to tossing a pancake if you are good at it try a race.

Did you know the lemon originated in China? Lemonade was a favourite of the chinese emperors.

Flip away it's Pancake Day!

33

February
Facts & Legends

Saraswati Puja 2nd February. A Hindu festival celebrating the goddess Saraswati and the first day of spring. Saraswati is goddess of music, poetry, dance and drama. This is a big festival especially in north India. People wear a lot of yellow to symbolise spring and warmth.

Imbolc Celtic Festival

The Celtic feast of "Imbolc" was the second of the 4 fire festivals on the pagan calendar. It symbolises the beginning of spring. A woman called Brighid, the daughter of Daga, a pagan god, was pregnant with the seed of the sun and was ripe with the promise of spring. Imbolc means in milk; think of lambs. Pagans used to pour milk over the ground.

Parinirvana is full moon day. It is the Buddhist celebration to remember the death of Buddha. On the day, the lights are dimmed for prayer and meditation and then later in the day the lights are brighter to show Buddha's teachings still illuminate the world.

Leap Years. Hundreds of years ago we had no leap years, but it was started to align the solar calendar and the 365 days calendar. It is one day women can propose to men thanks to St Patrick and St Bridget.

Groundhog Day

The second day of February is often called Groundhog Day. The old story goes that the Groundhog comes out of his hole to look for his shadow. If there is sunshine and he sees his shadow and goes back to sleep, there will be more winter, but if he doesn't then spring time will begin. There is an old German proverb about a badger looking out in the same way.

Shrove Tuesday is the day before the 40 days of Lent begin. It's a chance to use up food before fasting. Pancakes are traditional in Britain. Races began in 1445 when a woman making pancakes, realised she was late for church and dashed off taking her pan with her!

Snowdrops

Snowdrops are also known as candlemas bells, and are a symbol of hope. Adam and Eve were banished to a frozen barren land after they misbehaved in the Garden of Eden, but God had a change of heart and showed them fresh life and hope by sending in an angel who could turn snowflakes into snowdrops. Showing spring will always come after a harsh winter.

Candlemas

Candlemas marks the mid-point of winter. It is still noted in the Christian calendar as a time when all the candles used by a church for the year are brought to the church for blessings before being locked away. For Christians, candles are the symbol of the light Jesus brought to the world and he is their guiding light now.

Heavy Snowfall in 1855

A very strange thing happened on 8th February 1855. During the night in Devon, a really heavy snowfall blanketed the towns and countryside. People huddled beneath their bedclothes to help keep warm until morning. When they came out of their houses to see the bleak landscape they saw thousands of mystery footprints of a cloven hoof all moving in single file. They covered a distance of over 100 square miles and went through fields, rooftops, gardens and town. Everyone became a bit frightened when there was no explanation from experts, but the snow melted and even to this day it remains a mystery.

March

Oranges and Lemons

Oranges and lemons
  Say the bells of St Clement's
You owe me five farthings
  Say the bells of St Martin's
When will you pay me?
  Say the bells of Old Bailey
When I grow rich
  Say the bells of Shoreditch
When will that be?
  Say the bells of Stepney
I'm sure I don't know
  Says the great bell at Bow
Here comes a candle to light you to bed
  Here comes a chopper to chop off your head
Chip chop chip chop the last man's dead!

3rd month

March's flower is the Daffodil | *March's gemstone is the Aquamarine* | *March is named after the god Mars*

MON	TUES	WED	THURS	FRI	SAT	SUN
Oranges and Lemons Day **31**					St David's Day **1**	Mothering Sunday Simnel Sunday Dr Seuss, author. Born 1904 **2**
Holi (Hindu) Alexander Bell, telephone inventor. Born 1847 **3**	**4**	St Piran's Day (Cornwall) **5**	Maha Shivaratri (Hindu) Michelangelo, painter. Born 1475 **6**	**7**	International Women's Day Plant a Flower Day **8**	Passion Sunday (Christian) Cheesefare Sunday (Orthodox Christian) **9**
Commonwealth Day **10**	Penny Loaf Day (Nottinghamshire) **11**	**12**	Pi Day Albert Einstein, physicist. Born 1899 **13**	Julius Caesar, assassinated. 44BC **15**	**14**	Palm Sunday (Christian) **16**
St Patrick's Day **17**	**18**	St Joseph's Day 1st lunar eclipse recorded by humans (Babylon) 721 BC **19**	Maundy Thursday (Christian) 1st Day of Spring **20**	**Good Friday** Purim (Jewish) Holi (Hindu) **21**	World Water Day English football league formed 1888 **22**	Easter Sunday (Christian) Pakistan Day **23**
Easter Monday Harry Houdini, magician. Born 1874 **24**	Lady Day Slave Trade abolished 1807 **25**	**26**	**27**	**28**	Hindu Spring New Year Oxford and Cambridge Boat Race. London **29**	British summer time begins (clocks go forward 1 hour) Van Gogh, painter. Born 1853 **30**

Pisces 20th February – 20th March

Aries 21st March – 20th April

Hi Jago

I am staying with my friend
Esther at the moment she's named
after a queen. Today we are going
to her synagogue in fancy dress to
celebrate Purim we've got to make
loads of noise and every time we
hear Haman's name mentioned we
have to be even noisier afterwards
apparently we get delicious sweets
and goodies sounds fab.

lots of love Polly

Jago Harris

204 Latimer Road

London W10 6QY

Hi Polly

At school today our teacher miss Anna
had us make marbles as they did in
the old days — out of round stones,
hazelnuts, round balls of baked clay
even old cherry stones. max even
had a go at rolling eggs, my hazelnuts
went the furthest. miss Anna said it's
was a game played through lent like
skipping.

See you soon   Jago x

Polly Loughney

Honeysuckle Cottage

Lower Baldridge
Oxon OX8 4PT

Legendary Leprechaun Marionette

Other Ideas

Butterfly

*

1. Trace or photocopy the templates on this page. Stick them on to card, and cut them out.

2. Colour them in and use the hole punch to punch out the larger circles on the shoulders, hips and ends of arms and legs. Where the little circles are, push the tip of a pen through to make some smaller holes.

3. Attach the arms to the top of the body using the brass connectors and do the same for the legs. With the cotton, thread it through the little holes from front to back, across the back of the marionette and out through the front of the other side.

4. Do the same for the legs. Put the leprechaun face down and tie another piece of string from the middle of the top cotton down to the bottom piece of cotton and leave the rest dangling. Turn the little fellow over and check his arm and leg joints move freely with the connectors and then hang him up by his hat.

5. Pull the string at the bottom and his arms and legs should begin to dance.

Clown

*

Fairy

*

You will need

Brass paper connectors, thick card, pens and coloured pencils, tracing paper, cotton, hole punch, string.

Delicious Irish Stew

What to do

Ask the butcher to chop the middle neck of lamb into chops. Cut the potatoes and the onions into rings about 1cm thick. In our kitchen we have a big crock pot you can put on top or inside the oven, but if you haven't got one, you can use a saucepan with a metal handle. Seal the chops by quickly frying them on each side. Layer up potatoes, onions and the lamb chops. Then make another layer of the same with a pinch of salt and pepper between each layer, but finish the layering up with a layer of potatoes. Half cover the layers with water and put the pan or crock pot on top of the stove and bring the liquid up to the boil. This is when there are a lot of bubbles popping all the way around the potatoes and in the middle too. Turn down the temperature when it reaches boiling point and let it simmer for a long time, about 2 hours should do it. The meat and the potatoes become really tender and very tasty. We like to finish the pot off in the oven to make the top of the potatoes a bit crunchy, but you don't have to do that. It's ready to serve now, so chop a large handful of parsley and scatter it all over the top. This will feed 4 hungry people.

Ingredients

500g of middle neck of lamb or mutton
(older sheep)
1 kilo of potatoes
2 large onions
salt and pepper
chopped parsley
1 oven-proof dish or
saucepan with a metal handle

Irish stews used to be cooked in cauldron like pots on the coals.

Parsley contains three times as much vitamin C as oranges, twice as much iron as spinach, is rich in vitamin A and contains folate, potassium and calcium.

Dad made this for supper on St Patrick's Day.

Easter Eggheads

1 Crack the eggs towards the top and empty the white and yolk from them.

2 In the bottom of each egg shell pack in the compost up to halfway.

3 Scatter in the cress or mustard seeds and water them. Then sprinkle a little more compost over the top. We used different seed varieties to give different hair dos.

4 While the seeds start to grow, take your time and begin to decorate the egg shells. Funny faces and jazzy clothes are the best.

You will need

Eggs – as many as you like, paints, crayons, 1kg of compost soil, mustard and cress seeds, water.

Easter Lollipops

1. Start by melting your chocolate. Microwave it, or put it in a bowl over a pan of simmering water.

2. When there are no lumps left and you have shiny, runny chocolate, leave it to cool down for a bit.

3. Meanwhile, spread out the silicone paper on a board or tray. Pour the cooled chocolate into puddles on the paper, and shake it slightly to even it out.

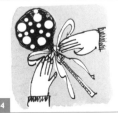

4. Push in the lolly stick and then sprinkle on the decorations. Pop the tray into the fridge to set and then decorate the stick with a ribbon bow.

You will need

Lolly sticks (or disposable chopsticks), chocolate (white, dark or milk), edible decorations (like little sugared eggs or edible flowers), ribbons, silicone paper.

Juicy Boiled Orange Cake

What to do

Pre-heat the oven to gas mark 7 or 225°C.
This cake is super easy to make. Once they've been baked they keep for weeks if you haven't eaten them by then. Boil the oranges whole in a pan of water until they are very soft, and leave them to cool down in the water so they stay juicy. You could do this the day before and leave the oranges in the fridge to get really cold. Next whizz the oranges in a food processor. If you don't have one, smash the oranges up with a potato masher so they get really mushy and then push them through a sieve to take out any chunks. Once you have your cold orange puree, put it in a mixing bowl with all the other ingredients and stir it all together really well. Tip this mixture into the 12" cake tin lined with parchment paper and spread it out evenly. Bake this cake in a gas mark 7 oven or 225°C, until the middle feels quite springy when you gently push the top. You could make this mixture into little cakes in muffin trays. One of the nice fresh things you can serve with this cake is a splodge of natural yoghurt and some fresh pomegranate seeds.

Ingredients

2 large oranges
6 eggs
225g of ground almonds
225g of golden caster sugar
1 teaspoon of baking powder
1 x 12" cake tin
baking parchment

Ruth's fabulous Passover cake

A great recipe as a Jewish Passover celebration cake as it has no raising agent.

Oranges are one of nature's best super foods. Packed with masses of disease-fighting nutrients, all tucked under the skin.

March
Facts & Legends

Simnel Sunday
Simnel Sunday is the 4th Sunday in Lent when simnel cakes are eaten. The marzipan balls on the top represent the 12 apostles, and 1 extra for Jesus.

Lent Lily
Lent Lily is one of the flowers associated with March and is also known as Narcissus or wild daffodil. It was named after the Greek boy, Narcissus in mythology. He was a vain boy always looking into the river at his reflection. One day he fell in and turned into a wild daffodil.

The Jewish festival of Purim usually happens in March. It is held on the day corresponding to the 14th day of Adar on the Hebrew calendar.

Palm Sunday is the beginning of the religious week of Easter. It marks the time when Jesus died on the cross. The holiday can move depending on the moon, and is also known as a movable feast.

The Easter Story
For Christians, Easter celebrates the resurrection of Jesus. The Easter week begins with Palm Sunday, when Jesus arrived in Jerusalem. Spy Wednesday commemorates Judas who betrayed Jesus.

Maundy Thursday comes from a Latin word "to command" which Jesus did at the last supper. Good Friday was the day Jesus was put to death. Easter Sunday remembers his resurrection and Monday celebrates his going to heaven to be with God, his father.

Oranges and Lemons
100's of years ago, barges carrying oranges and lemons, landed near the church of St Clements Dane. At the end of March, children went to the church service, sang the famous rhyme and were given an orange and lemon.

Lady Mabella Tichborne

Poor Lady Mabella Tichborne lay on her sick bed dying, when she asked her husband to provide a gift of bread for all the people arriving for the feast of the Annunciation and after she had died.

Her horrible husband Roger, said he would give the same amount of flour that could be milled, from as much of the land as she could walk around before a burning log went out. She was a determined lady and had to crawl around the land. She was so sick her husband didn't think she would do it, but she managed to crawl all the way, and just as she arrived back at his feet, the log flickered out.

Hercules Clay

For three nights a man called Hercules Clay dreamed that he saw his house on fire. He was so worried about it he moved his family out, and just as he had left his house a bomb was fired by the parliamentarians during the British Civil War, and it destroyed the house. He really had a lucky escape, so he left £100 pounds to provide penny loaves for the poor.

April

April Fool's Day

"April Fool's a-comin' and you're the biggest
fool a-runnin'."

"April Fool's past, and you're the biggest fool
at last."

"April Fool's has come and gone; who's the fool that
carried it on?"

4th month

April's flower is the Sweet Pea

April's gemstone is the Diamond

April is named after the Roman goddess Aphrodite

MON	TUES	WED	THURS	FRI	SAT	SUN
	April Fool's Day **1**	Hans Christian Andersen, author. Born 1805 **2**	Jane Goodall, biologist. Born 1934 **3**	**4**	Pocahontas got married 1640 **5**	Daffodil Sunday National Tartan Day **6**
World Health Day **7**	Astronomy Day Hanamatsuri (Buddhas birthday) Picasso, painter. Died 1973 **8**	Isambard Brunel, engineer. Born 1806 **9**	**10**	**11**	London Marathon Yuri Gagarin 1st flight into space 1961 **12**	Nepalese New Year Baisakhi or Vaisakhi (Indian festival) **13**
Titanic Struck iceberg (Night) 1912 **14**	Swallows Day Leonardo Da Vinci, painter. Born 1452 **15**	Charlie Chaplin, actor. Born 1889 **16**	**17**	**18**	**19**	1st Day of Passover (Pesach) (Jewish) **20**
Queen Elizabeth II Born 1926 **21**	Earth Day Lenin Day, political leader. Born 1870 **22**	St George's Day Slay a Dragon Day William Shakespeare, poet and playwright. Died 1613 **23**	Hubble Telescope launched into the earth's orbit 1990 **24**	Cuckoo Day Anzac Day Oliver Cromwell, Born 1599 **25**	End of Passover (Pesach) (Jewish) **26**	**27**
28	Walpurgis Night **29**	**30**				

Aries 21st March – 20th April.

Taurus 21st April – 21st May

Hi Jago

I Hope you are well. My cousin
Jim has been training to run
the London marathon — it's this
weekend so we are all going
up to London to cheer him on.
Once people didn't believe it was
possible for a human to run such a
distance.

lots of love Polly XX

Jago Harris

204 Latimer Road

London W10 6QY

Hi Polly

Guess what? I played a trick on dad
today he came down for breakfast
wanting a boiled egg, I turned my
eaten one upside down and gave
it to him April fool — tee hee
hee hee pinch punch first of the
month white rabbits no returns.

Love Jago

Polly Loughney

Honeysuckle Cottage

Lower Baldridge
Oxon OX8 4PT

Family Tree

You will need to talk to some of the older members of your family to find out who your ancestors were. You could also have a look on the internet to find some things out too.

1 Begin by sorting out family photographs of the last 3 generations of your family.

2 Paint a tree on the card, let it dry and start to position the photos.

3 Place the grandpas and grandmas at the top. Write their names, birthdays and the date they got married.

4 Under them, draw lines down and put photos of your daddy under his parents and your mummy under her parents. You can include pictures of your aunts and uncles next to them. Now write in their birthdays.

5 Draw a line between your mummy and daddy and write the date they got married. Under your mummy and daddy draw a line down and put your photo in. If you have brothers and sisters, stick them next to you. Include your birthdays aswell.

6 You could include pets, or cousins if you like. It depends how big your family or your tree is.

You will need

Family photos, scissors, card, sticky tape, 1 black pen, pens, pencils, crayons.

Grandmas' Shepherd's Pie

What to do

Turn on the oven to gas 7 or 220°C. Boil and mash the potatoes with butter and milk. Add some salt and pepper. Chop the onion and carrot up as small as you can, and start to fry them in the vegetable oil. When they begin to go golden brown, add the minced lamb, and stir it together with some stock and the chopped parsley and let it simmer slightly in the pan. Season with salt and pepper. Give this 10 minutes to cook together, then pile the meat mixture into your serving dish and dollop the potatoes on top. Spread the potato out with a spoon until there's a good even layer on top and mark it like plough furrows with a fork. Put this dish in the oven for about 20 to 30 minutes and let it go golden brown on top.

Ingredients

500g of potatoes
30g butter
30ml milk
salt and pepper
30ml vegetable oil
1 onion
2 carrots
sprig of thyme
300g of minced lamb
stock cube in 400ml of water
a handful of chopped parsley
1 oven-proof dish for baking
the pie in

Tea with Georgie, Ben and Tashie

Did you know carrot leaves were used as fashionable accents on hats by chic nobles in the court of king James the first of England.

Shepherd's pie is a great recipe for using up leftover roast lamb – if you use minced beef this would be a cottage pie rather than a shepherd's pie.

53

Swords and Shields

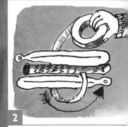

You will need

2 large sheets of
cardboard, 1 roll of tin foil,
2 pieces of paper, ballpoint
pen, 1 old newspaper,
sticky tape, paper clips,
4m of braid or string,
glue stick, paints.

Draw a blade and handle on card and cut it out twice. In the middle of each blade, score a straight line lengthways with a ballpoint pen and pinch the card together.

Cut a piece of newspaper as long as the blade and roll it up into a tight tube. Stick this to the inside of one of the blades. Put the other blade over the top and stick them together with sticky tape.

Smother one side of the blade with a glue stick and glue a piece of foil, shiny side up, to it. Tuck over the edges and turn over the blade. Glue more foil to this side and trim off the edges.

Fold a thick piece of paper in half and draw a shape for the handguard. Cut out both layers and glue foil to them.

Glue the handguard around the blade and hold it together with paper clips. You can press a design in to the handguard with the pen if you like.

Finally wind the braid around the handle of your sword which you can glue into place. Leave it to dry for a while before you begin to battle!

Did you know?

Some swords are really famous and are given names. How many can you think of? Excaliber, the sword belonging to king Arthur is probably the most famous.

Knights were very brave, and were awarded coats of arms. They used to decorate the front of their shield with it, and their opponent would know who they were fighting. They followed a "code of chivalry", which meant they had to behave well at all times even during fighting.

Fleur-de-lis is the French for lily flower. The French royal family used it as their badge.

Knights did a lot of protecting the king and queen and their castle. Sometimes the enemy found sneaky ways into the castle using gutters or waste tunnels.

Swords were made of metal folded 100's of times to make it very strong and sharp, and shields were made of wood, and used to protect the knight from other knights' swords.

Kings and knights used to have huge banquets to celebrate battles and show off how rich and powerful they were.

For the shield

Fold the paper in half and draw half a shield against the fold. Cut it out and draw around it on to the cardboard. Cut out the cardboard.

Cut the paper shield into four and paint them with your favourite colour. Paint your cardboard shield your second favourite colour. Glue two opposite pieces of paper on to the card shield and leave it to dry. You can make a design for your shield. Have a look at our designs.

Cut two strips of cardboard the length of the shield. Stick them to the back of the shield with sticky tape. Put your arms through the loops and now you are ready for battle!

Some Shield Designs

Rhubarb Fool for an April Fool

What to do

Cut the rhubarb into 4cm sticks and give them a wash to get rid of any soil or grit. Tip them into a saucepan with 75g of the sugar, the vanilla pod which needs to be split with a knife to let the little black seeds come out, the zest and juice of the orange and a little splash of water (about 30ml). Put this pan on top of the stove and bring the rhubarb up to boiling point, stirring it every so often to stop the sugar burning in patches. Let the rhubarb simmer for a further 5 – 10 minutes or until tender when you push a knife into it. Take the pan off the heat and tip the fruit into something cold to help it cool down quite quickly. In another bowl, pour in the cream, add the rest of the sugar and begin to whisk it. You can go electric if you like, but we enjoy using a balloon whisk. It gives us big muscles and stops us whisking it too much and making butter!

When the cream is forming soft peaks, or what we call floppy points, stop whisking and add two thirds of the cold cooked rhubarb and the carton of custard and stir it all together gently. In the glasses or glass bowl, put a good splodge of rhubarb in and then some of the creamy mixture. You can make as many layers as you like or just put some of the rhubarb at the top and bottom. If the fool is for a special occasion you can decorate it with things you might like on cupcakes, like silver sugar balls, toasted almonds or rose petals. It's up to you. It's also quite nice to eat with a biscuit like shortbread or biscotti for a bit of crunch.

Ingredients

1 vanilla pod
100g golden caster sugar
500g rhubarb
grated zest and juice of 1 orange
500ml double cream
500ml carton of custard
6 pretty glasses to serve them in
or 1 big glass bowl

Rhubarb fool race - JoJo won!

We've used rhubarb in our fool - you could try gooseberry, blackcurrants or apricot to name a few others.

Did you know rhubarb is actually a vegetable. Mostly it's used as a fruit though don't try and eat it raw!

April
Facts & Legends

The Romans called the month Aprilis. It may come from the word meaning to open, as in the buds of spring and all the leaves which begin to open in April. Alternatively it could relate to the Greek goddess of love, Aphrodite.

April Fool's Day

In 1752 Pope Gregory decided to change the Christian calendar to the Gregorian calendar, making January the first month of the year rather than April. Some people forgot and so they were called the April fools. Jokes are nowadays played before midday on the 1st April. Jewish people believe the custom of making April fools came from the story that Noah sent out his dove on the 1st of April.

Passover is also known as Pesach – a really important Jewish festival. In the bible, it refers to the story of the plague in Egypt. God protected people if the blood of a lamb was put on the lintel of the door to their house.

Small animals that hibernate are usually coming out of their burrows in April. The birds fly back northwards and the bees and butterflies begin to collect nectar from the first flowers of the season.

William Shakespeare

was baptised on the 26th of April 1564, but no one knows when his birthday actually was. He is thought to be the most famous playwright in the world, he wrote 38 plays and 154 sonnets or poems. When he was 18 he married Anne Hathaway. He worked from 1590-1612 and was really popular with Queen Elizabeth the 1st. Have you heard of Romeo and Juliet, Macbeth or Hamlet? He wrote them all proving he could write amazing comedies and tradgedy which may be why he is still so popular today.

Titanic was an olympic class passenger liner, that sadly hit an iceberg on april 14th and sank on april 15th 1912. She weighed 46,328 tons and could carry 3547 people in total. It took 3 years to build her. She tragically sank on her maiden voyage.

St George's Day

The 23rd of April is St George's Day. He is the patron saint of scouting and of England. It is said he once saved a village from great danger. All the villagers were frightened of a fierce dragon that lived close by, so George went on his charger and killed the dragon with his sword.

It is essential to be very brave if you are a knight, like George was. You should have a "charger" or horse, be good at jousting, serve the King or Queen with true honour and rescue damsels in distress.

Walpurgis Night

On the evening of the 30th of April, numerous rituals are performed to ward off evil. Walpurgis was the name of a woman who was born in Britain around 700AD. She was an abbess at a Catholic convent and was made a saint the day after she died in 779AD.

Walpurgis night became a festival to drive out evil spirits. Pagans of this time used to perform Viking-style fertility celebrations in April and May, so the days have become intertwined, with May Day festivities, maypoles, morris dancing and hobby horses.

May

Hurray for May Day! – sung to "London Bridge"

May Day's here with sun so bright,
sun so bright, sun so bright.
May Day's here with sun so bright.
Hurray for May Day!

May Day's here with flowers in bloom,
flowers in bloom, flowers in bloom.
May Day's here with flowers in bloom.
Hurray for May Day!

May's flower is the Lily of the Valley   May's gemstone is the Emerald   May is named after the Roman goddess Maia

MON	TUES	WED	THURS	FRI	SAT	SUN
			📖 May Day ✂ Garland Day Ascension Day 1	Yom Ha Sho'ah (Jewish) 2	1st aeroplane landed at North Pole 1952 3	Space Day 4
May Day Amy Johnson flies solo England to Australia. 1930 5	Roger Bannister ran the 4 min/mile. 1954 Penny Black, 1st stamp 1840 6	7	Yom Ha Atzma'int (Jewish) V.E. Day in Europe Buddha's Birthday 8	Europe Day 9	10	Pentecost – Whit Sunday (Christian) 11
Whit Monday Nurses' Day Florence Nightingale, Nurse. Born 1820 12	13	14	15	16	17	1st Wimpy restaurant opened 1955 18
St Dunstans Day 19	✂ Flower Day 20	21	Corpus Christi Day Laurence Olivier, actor. Born 1907 22	Lag B'Omer (Jewish) 23	Africa Day 24	Arbor tree Day 25
Spring Holiday 📖 Cheese Rolling Day 26	27	Ian Flemming, writer of James Bond. Born 1908 28	📖 Oak Apple Day Hillary and Norgay, 1st to reach top of Everest. 1953 29	Joan of Arc Died 14/31 30	31	

Taurus 21st April – 21st May

Gemini 22nd May – 21st June

Dear Jago,

Today we went round gran's garden picking pretty flowers for our mayday garland — we made one each and wore them all day — m'y sister even wore hers in the bath because she didn't want to take it off — ah! Big kiss.

lots of love Polly XX

Jago Harris

204 Latimer Road

London W10 6QY

Hi Polly

Did you know that on the 3rd of may 1952 the first aeroplane landed at the north pole.

mum says it is really beautiful but really cold out there, with lots of ice and Polar bears.

x x from Jago

Polly Loughney

Honeysuckle Cottage

Lower Baldridge
Oxon OX8 4PT

Flower Garland Necklace

Other Ideas

Why don't you try some other things?

Here are some ideas:

*

Beads

*

Pasta

*

Corks

*

Leaves

*

Or plastic flowers if you can't find such pretty flowers

1. Begin by making a hole in the centre of each of the flowers.

2. Snip the straws into 3cm long pieces.

3. Tie a big loose knot at one end of the yarn and then thread the needle at the other end.

4. Start to thread a flower followed by a bead, a piece of straw, a bead and another flower. Start with a bead again and keep threading until you run out of yarn or flowers.

5. Take both ends of the string and tie the knot so you can tie both ends together and make a large loop.

6. You can wear this like a gigantic necklace or you can leave it as one long string and use it like bunting or wrap it around things to decorate them.

You will need

1 large embroidery needle, 1m of thick yarn or thin string, 10 colourful drinking straws, scissors, 30 real or artificial flowers like daisies, roses or lilies and 60 beads.

Bright and Bold Baby Vegetable Salad

What to do

Prepare all the baby vegetables by trimming off any hairy roots and cutting the leaves down. Don't peel them otherwise you lose a lot of vegetable and flavour. Bring a large pan of water up to the boil and salt it. When the water is at a rolling boil, add the vegetables and turn the temperature down slightly to a simmer. After about 6 or 7 minutes, take a little knife and push it into the vegetables to see if they are tender. If they are hard, give them a few minutes longer. When they are tender, drain them into a colander and leave them to cool down. We splash cold water on ours. It helps to keep the colours very bright. Next wash all of the lettuce leaves in cold water and leave them to drain in a sieve or another colander. In a mixing bowl put the mustard, sugar, salt and pepper and balsamic together and whisk it all with a balloon whisk. Slowly start to add the olive oil, whisking all the time. This makes the dressing nice and thick, which will coat all of the salad ingredients nicely. When the vegetables are cold, add them to the leaves and dress them with a little of the dressing. Turn them gently together and then begin to pile them all up on a serving plate. You can serve the rest of the dressing on the side in a jug, so you have a little more if you like. This is so healthy and colourful. It will make you feel good just looking at it. You can add other things too, like croutons, or crumbled feta cheese. Even chicken or ham are tasty additions.

baby carrots
baby fennel
baby beetroot
baby leeks
baby turnips
a mixture of little salad leaves, little ruby
chard and young spinach
50ml good olive oil
50ml good balsamic vinegar
1 teaspoon of wholegrain mustard
1 teaspoon of sugar
salt and pepper

Most baby vegetables are actually fully ripe special miniature vegetables grown for perfection.

Sweet beet — beetroot has one of the highest sugar contents of any vegetable (it is a relative of sugar beet!)

Mum and her friends really like this

65

Miniature Garden

You will need

1 container or box to make garden in, 1 bin bag, some compost or soil, scissors, little plants, moss, twigs and things from your park or garden, little models of people and animals.

Take your container and line it with part of the bin bag. Then fill this with soil or compost. Give it a water.

Mark out your little garden, make some flower beds, maybe a pond or a verandah patio.

To make a pond, take a small piece of the left-over bin bag and make a little dip in the earth and line it with plastic. Surround the edge of your pond with little stones and fill it up with water.

We like to make the lawn in our garden with moss, but you could sow seeds if you prefer.

To make furniture, twist together some small twigs and weave them with string.

The flowers and plants we used are all snippets of big plants that look like tiny trees and bushes.

Did you know?

GROWING THINGS

Along with seeds from packets, there are other things you can find to try and grow in your garden or window box.

Have a go with an avocado stone. Get the papery brown skin off the stone and poke 3 holes around the middle of the stone. Stick a toothpick in each one and balance the stone, pointy end up, over a glass. Fill the glass with water and cover the bottom third of the stone. Put the glass somewhere warm and sunny and change the water every week. Very soon you will see the stone split and the roots will begin to grow. This is going to be your avocado tree sapling.

Find a sweet potato with a few knobbly buds on it. Stick 3 sticks around the middle as with the avocado, and sit it in a glass of water too. Top up the water every so often and change the water weekly. Again the roots and shoots should begin to grow. You can plant it in the garden and wait for a few months for more tubers to grow from these roots.

You could try cracking a peach stone and growing it in wet tissue paper, or pomegranate. What else can you think of to try growing? Would a tomato be worth trying?

Other Ideas

For fairies you could use: gliiter, tinsel, chimes and mirrors

*

For birds you could use: nests, little eggs, tiny feathers

*

For sculptures you could use: anything abstract!

Scrummy Scones

What to do

Turn the oven to gas mark **7** or **220°C** and whilst it heats up, sift the flour, bicarbonate of soda, cream of tartar and salt into a mixing bowl. Put the butter in the flour mix in little bits the size of blueberries, and then rub the flour and butter through your fingertips until all the butter has been "rubbed in". Add the milk altogether and mix it quite quickly with your hands until all the flour is made into a sloppy dough. Turn this on to a floured work surface and knead it briefly to a smoother dough. Once it makes this stop kneading, but just push the dough flatter with your fingers, until it's about 2.5cm thick and then start to cut out the rounds as close to each other as possible. Put these on to a baking tray and then into the oven. Don't put them too close to each other on the tray otherwise they may spread and join up. You may be able to re press the remaining mixture to get one or two more scones. They should take about 10 minutes to cook, and they go a lovely golden colour on the top.

We think it's best to eat them when they are still a bit warm, but they are still delicious later on. You can add some sultanas to the dough mix and scatter Demerara on top, if you like a sweet scone, or add cheddar and a little mustard powder if you prefer more savoury things. When we have scones at home, we make lots of different things to go on top. Clotted cream and jam is a favourite, but so is Nutella and banana. Crème Fraiche and smoked salmon or ham is really good too!

Ingredients

- 500g of plain flour
- 2 large pinches of salt
- 2 teaspoons of bicarbonate of soda
- 4 teaspoons of cream of tartar
- 90g of butter
- 300ml milk
- pastry cutter
- with a crinkly edge
- 1 baking sheet

Making scones at Max and Amber's house

Our scones are plain but you could try raisins, orange zest, cheese or tomatoes.

Scones — Which way do you make yours — cream first then jam or jam on first with cream on top?

Facts & Legends

Maia

Maia. The month may have been named after Maia, who was the Roman god of fertility. She was also known as bona dea. Her festival was in May.

May Day

May Day is a pagan holiday. First thing in the morning in May Day, young girls used to rush out into the garden to wash their faces in dew. The old tale says anyone who has washed his or her face in dew will have a wonderful complexion all year. May Day is also called Garland Day. Children used to collect greenery to decorate maypoles and to make crosses. Maypole dancing was a way of rejoicing, blessing trees and making ready for good growing.

Christopher Columbus

Christopher Columbus began his third world voyage 30th May 1498. His ship was called "La Niña" and carried provisions for 1 year. La Niña was 67 feet long, 21 feet wide and weighed 57 tones.

Chelsea pensioners

Chelsea pensioners parade in front of an officer and three cheers are given for Charles II who established the Royal Hospital as a home for old soldiers. His statue is decorated with oak leaves in memory of his escape.

Cheese Rolling

Cheese rolling is a very old tradition. At Coopers Hill, Brockworth, in Gloucestershire, this centuries-old tradition involves competitors chasing a rolling cheese down a three-in-one slope. The person who catches the cheese is allowed to keep it.

Winner!

St Dunstan's Day

St Dunstan's Day St Dunstan was an Anglo-Saxon saint who lived in Glastonbury over 1000 years ago. After being exiled by horrid king Eadwig, the kings successor made Dunstan, an archbishop. He planned the kings coronation with a ceremony still used today.

Oak Apple Day

This is the day that people wear oak leaves pinned to their clothes to remember that on May 29th King Charles II returned to London after the restoration of the monarchy in 1660. King Charles had hidden in an oak tree to escape capture from the Roundheads. Until the 20th century, anyone found not wearing an oak leaf or oak apple on May 29th could be kicked, pinched or otherwise abused, like maybe whipped with nettles.

Bring Home the Bacon

The saying really means to prove your worth. It comes from a tale told in 1104 when the lord of a manor, Reginald Fitzwater and his new wife dressed themselves as paupers and begged for the prior's blessing one year after their wedding. The prior was so touched by their devotion to each other he gave them a side of bacon, or "flitch". The lord revealed himself and promised land to the priory, with the condition that other devoted couples must be rewarded the same way. Chaucer mentions it in his stories and people still flock to Dunmow these days to celebrate the tradition.

June

Summer Solstice

The Summer solstice, the longest day of the year, when the sun is at its most northern point in the sky, is celebrated by people of many beliefs. On the longest day of the year people from across the country get together at Avebury and Stonehenge to celebrate the coming of summer.

Solstice comes from the Latin (*sol*, sun; *sistt*, stands still).

6th month

June's flower is the Rose | June's Gemstone is the Pearl | June is named after the Roman goddess Juno

MON	TUES	WED	THURS	FRI	SAT	SUN
Meteor Day **30**						International Children's Day **1**
National Day of Italy Coronation Day **2**	**3**	**4**	World Environment Day **5**	National Day of Sweden YMCA began in London 1844 **6**	Derby Day **7**	World Oceans Day **8**
Shavouot, Feast of Weeks (Jewish) St Columba's Day **9**	Maurice Sendak, author. Born 1928 **10**	Jacques Cousteau, oceanographer. Born 1910 **11**	Queen's official birthday Trooping of the colour **12**	**13**	World Flag Day **14**	Father's Day **15**
Valentina Tereshkova 1st woman in space 1963 **16**	**17**	**18**	Garfield's birthday **19**	British summer time begins **20**	**21**	**22**
23	Midsummer's Day **24**	Wimbledon begins **25**	**26**	**27**	**28**	**29**

Gemini 22nd May – 21st June

Cancer 22nd June – 23rd July

Hi Jago

Hope you are well do you play
tennis? Mum is a big Wimbledon
fan so it's a tennis month at
our house. I have been practising
my backhand and eating lots
of strawberries and cream in the
garden — yummy.

Love from Polly XX

Jago Harris

204 Latimer Road

London W10 6QY

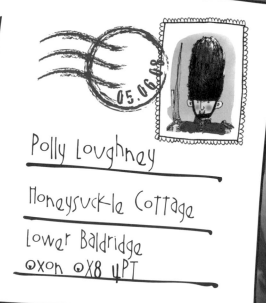

Hi Polly

Today was world Environment day. It
was really fun — we had to do four
good things for the environment mine
were not letting the tap run while
I was cleaning my teeth, walking to
school and back not using the car
planting some seeds in recycled yoghurt
pots and recycling all my food wrappers.

from Jago

Polly Loughney

Honeysuckle Cottage

Lower Baldridge
Oxon OX8 4PT

Frosted Rose Petals

Other Ideas

You can use different flowers like primroses and violets

*

They make a lovely present for someone special

*

They could be used as cake decorations

*

Try crystalising fruit. Grapes work very well.

1 Pick the rose petals apart and throw away any bruised ones.

2 Whisk the egg whites lightly and paint the rose petals lightly with it.

3 Sprinkle the petals with caster sugar and gently place them on the paper and then on the tray.

4 Pop these somewhere airy to dry out.

You will need

Rose petals, 3 egg whites, caster sugar, small paintbrush, baking tray, silicone paper.

Delicious
Father's Day Breakfast

What to do

Pre-heat the oven to gas mark 6 or 200°C.
Add the vegetable oil to a hot frying pan and begin by frying the cubes of pancetta and the sausage cut into 6 or 8 pieces. When they are brown and slightly crispy, add the cherry tomatoes, chopped-up potatoes and the mushrooms which should be cut in half. Let them go golden too.
Once you have a pan full of lovely golden breakfast bits, whisk the 4 eggs in a dish, and pour them into the pan over all the meat and vegetables. Stir this a little around the edges. It looks a bit like scrambled eggs for a while, and then let the mixture settle in the pan and make a bit of a crust. Next put the whole pan into the oven and let the eggs set on the top. In some countries this is called a tortilla or frittata. When the eggs have set, take the pan out of the oven and let it stand for about 10 minutes. While it settles, make the tea, toast the bread and prepare the tray you are going to put the breakfast on. Cut the omelette into wedges and lift them out on to a plate using a palette knife or cake slice. We like to serve it with baked beans and toast, but you could serve it with sautéed spinach or a salad.

Ingredients

30g diced pancetta or bacon
10 cherry tomatoes
5 button mushrooms
2 sausages
25ml vegetable oil
a handful of cooked potatoes
4 eggs
2 slices of bread for toast
salt and pepper
frying pan with a metal handle

Yummy - lucky daddy!

Did you know eggs contain the 7 essential amino acids humans need to survive?

You could also try a traditional english breakfast, american blueberry pancakes or even huevos rancheros.

Ocean Diorama

You will need

1 large box, string, coloured paper, glue, glitter, book of fishes, scissors, sticky tape, sparkly things to stick on.

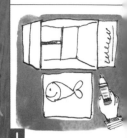

Take the box and open up one side of it. Cover the inside with paper that is the colour of the sea, or use a photograph of sea life. Next trace around some of the fishes in the book you would like to use and cut them out.

We then traced around them on to coloured card and decorated each one with a face and some glitter. For the octopus we added some sparkly sequins to look like suckers and for the clam we added a pearl inside the shell.

We labelled all of our fishes to help us remember about them and on the back we wrote a few facts about each fish. Poke a hole into the top of all of the fish and thread through the string.

Push holes through the top of the box and begin to thread the strings through. We found out how deep some of the fishes live in the ocean and then suspended them in stages that matched those facts.

If you put this box in a breeze the fish move around slightly.

Other things for dioramas
Birds
Bugs
Aeroplanes and other aircraft.

Did you know?

All the seas on earth cover 71% of its surface.

97% of all the earth's water is saltwater.

There is the deepest underwater valley in the world in the Pacific, called the Mariana Trench – it's about 11,000m deep (Mount Everest is only 8,848m).

The longest mountain range is actually underwater in the Arctic ocean down to the middle of the Atlantic and into the Pacific.

There is a man called Jacques Mayol, who could dive the deepest without any help from breathing equipment. His record is 282 feet.

The largest waterfall on earth is underwater. It is in the Denmark Strait and slowly cascades over 2 miles down. It's 3 times bigger than Angel Falls in Venezuela, which is the tallest land waterfall.

Wibbly Wobbly Sunset Jelly

What to do

Add 100ml to the juice of the 4 oranges. Purée the raspberries by mashing them and pushing them through a sieve to get rid of all the pips and then add 100ml of water to the purée. In 2 separate pans heat up the orange and the raspberry mix, but don't boil them. You can use a microwave to do this if you like. The juices should be too hot to touch but not bubbling. Soak the gelatine in a little extra water until it softens and then split it between the 2 juices. Stir them until the gelatine is totally dissolved and then taste each mix. We think the orange takes very little alteration but the raspberry is sometimes really sour and we need to add some sugar. Make it taste good to you. If you like it really sweet, keep adding the sugar.

Let these mixtures cool down, and with the raspberry mix, fill the bottom of your glasses with about 1cm of liquid. Put them in the fridge to set before adding the orange layer in the same way. Keep setting them in the fridge and adding more layers until you have a stripy jelly. We add a cake sparkler to the top of ours and light them when they go to the table. Once you've eaten a good spoon out of each glass you could put in some ice cream or sorbet.

Ingredients

4 oranges juiced
300g fresh raspberries (you can cheat
and use orange juice or raspberry
purée bought in sachets)
6 leaves of golden gelatine
200ml water
sugar to taste
some pretty glasses
or a mould to set the jelly in

Chloe helping with sprinkles stuck all over her!

Wibble wobble wibble wobble jelly on a plate.

Gelatine is not vegetarian but you can buy a vegetarian alternative called agaragar made out of seaweed.

June
Facts & Legends

Well dressing. This tradition involves the decoration of springs and wells with pictures made from living plants and flowers. It began to bless the water for the people using it. It is followed in Buxton and Bakewell, Derbyshire.

Beltane Festival

This pagan festival marks the return of summer. People lit large fires and burned their winter bedding, before making new hay mattresses. It is an ancient Celtic ceremony that has been celebrated throughout Europe for thousands of years. It is written that King James himself witnessed this festival in the 15th century. The festival culminates with the crowning of the Beltane queen.

St Columba's Day

Columba was born in Ireland, into the Royal clan of Donegal about 1500 years ago. He left Ireland to spread the word of God. In 563 he landed in Scotland at Iona, where he and 12 others, built a monastry. Many followers lived with him.

Midsummer's Eve, at midnight, young women should scatter petals, say a poem and wait for their true loves to find them the next day. This is the longest day of the year, it's been known for witches and fairies to weave their magic.

The Druid Ceremony

These ceremonies happen all over England on Summer Solstice. The main ceremony happens at Stonehenge in Wiltshire. On the night before midsummer, a group of white-robed druids gather to watch the sun rise. As it does it rises exactly over the heel stone, one of the stones that lie outside the main circle at Stonehenge.

Appleby Horse Fair, Westmorland is is known for its gypsy fair. Here traveller families celebrate their history, music, folklore and family relationships they also trade and barter in livestock. It was established in 1685 under King James II.

St John's Wort

With the coming of Christianity, many pagan midsummer festivities were moved to the feast of St John the Baptist. People would light their bonfires on the eve and stay up until midnight to welcome in the following day. It is a time for magic and mystery. Evil spirits were said to appear and people gathered herbs and flowers to protect themselves. One of the most powerful plants was known as chase devil, which is now know as St John's Wort. People used it to make potions and in garlands, believing this would shield them from evil spirits. Herbalists use this nowadays to help with stress and depression.

The Trooping of the Colour

The official birthday of the sovereign is marked every year by a colourful and historic military parade, known as the trooping of the colour. The origin of the ceremony dates back to the early 18th century when the colours of the battalion served as rallying points in battle. In 1748 it was decided that the parade would also mark the official birthday of the sovereign. Soldiers on parade, have to remain totally still unless they are marching. It gets very hot sometimes, and some poor soldiers faint with the heat in their dress uniforms.

July

Independence Day

In the United States, Independence Day is a holiday celebrating America's independence as a nation - it happened on July 4, 1776. Independence Day is commonly associated with fireworks, parades, barbecues, beer, picnics, baseball games and special events celebrating the history, government, and traditions of the United States.

7th month

July's flower is the Larkspur   July's gemstone is the Ruby   July is named after Julius Caesar

MON	TUES	WED	THURS	FRI	SAT	SUN
		Halfway point of the year. Henley Royal Regatta begins **1**	The Mallard broke the record for steam engines at 128 mph 1938 **2**	Independence Day (US) **3**	Family Day. Tynwald Day (Isle of Man) **4**	**5**
6						
7	**8**	Vintner's Procession (City of London) **9**	**10**	St Benedict's Day **11**	Battle of Boyne Day Orange mens' Day (Ireland) **12**	National Day (Northern Ireland) **13**
14	St Swithin's Day **15**	Ratha Yatra (Hindu) **16**	**17**	**18**	National stick your tongue out Day **19**	St Margaret's Day 1st Lunar Landing US Astronaut Neil Amstrong 1969 **20**
21	**22**	**23**	Amelia Eurhart, aviator. Born 1897 **24**	English oyster season begins. St James Day St Christopher's Day **25**	George Bernard Shaw, playwright. Born 1856 **26**	**27**
1st potatoes from Columbia arrived 1586 **28**	**29**	**30**	JK Rowling, author. Born 1965 **31**			

Cancer 22nd June – 23rd July

Leo 24th July – 23rd August

Hi Jago

I hope you are well - I am in Florida with my Uncle Bill for our summer holiday we are going to Disney Epcot centre and then afterwards going to an Independence day party apparently there will be lots of bbq's and picnics. Sounds fab. Have a nice day.

Polly

04.07.08

Jago Harris

204 Latimer Road

London W10 6QY

Hi Polly
I hope you are having a great holiday. School holidays are lovely, lots of lazy days in the garden with my friends. Today we had a competition to see who could stick their tongue out the furthest for national stick your tongue out day! Think Chloe won.
xx Jago

19.07.08

Polly Loughney

Honeysuckle Cottage

Lower Baldridge
Oxon OX8 4PT

Tie Dye T-shirts

1. Lay out the t-shirt flat and light the candle. Dribble the melting wax on to the t-shirt. We've done crossed bones on our design. Leave the wax to set.

2. Position your corks in 3 different areas and bunch up the t-shirt around it. Tie it with string as tightly as you can. This will stop the dye reaching all of the t-shirt.

3. In the bucket, mix the dye according to directions and plunge in the t-shirt. Let the liquid filter through, and leave the t-shirt for 24 hours.

4. Take the t-shirt out of the dye and untie the string to release the corks and "wow" you should have a really jazzy design!

5. The dye can't work where the wax is. Scrape off the wax where you can and then with a hot iron put the newspaper over the wax and iron it. The paper will absorb the hot wax.

6. Ahh harr – you have a tie-dye batik pirate shirt, me hearty!! Give it a wash before you wear it, or else you'll go blue too!

You could try tie dyeing all sorts of different things;

*

Other bits of clothing you have around such as pyjamas or pants or how about a sheet which you could use as a sail or as a tent.

*

You will need

1 plain white t-shirt, 1 cold colour dye, 1 wax canadle, 3 corks, 1 ball of string, 1 bucket, cold water.

Pirate's Picnic

What to do

First make the egg mayonnaise, put the eggs on to boil for 8 minutes and then plunge them into cold water. This stops them going grey around the edge of the yolk. When the eggs are cold, peel the shell, then grate them on a cheese grater into a bowl and then add the mayonnaise. Mix well together and add some salt and pepper. Cut the cress from the punnet, and add it to the egg. Cut the shape of a treasure map out of the tortilla wraps, have a look at ours for an idea, and then spread the egg mix on one side and finish it off with the other tortilla. Use a cake decorating pen to write on top and you are ready to eat it now. For the cutlass kebabs, cut the pineapple into wedges that are about 2 cm thick on the outside, going into a point in the middle. Wash the grapes and the berries, and take the hull out of the strawberries. Thread the fruit onto the skewers. Push some grapes and blueberries on to start with. These will make the jewelled handle for your cutlass. After about 6 or 7 grapes and blueberries, carefully push the large slice of pineapple on and finish it off with a strawberry. Now you are ready to pack these into a tub for eating on the picnic.

Ingredients

floured tortillas
sliced ham x 5 slices
butter
cress x 1 punnet
2 hard-boiled eggs
2 large spoons of mayonnaise
watercress
12 bamboo skewers
1 bunch of green grapes
blueberries and strawberries
1 pineapple

Pirate Oscar eating his cutlass

Why are pirates called pirates?

Because they aargh!!

Some piratey activities to try:
- organise a treasure hunt.
- make an eye patch.
- see who can shout pieces of 8 or ahoy my hearties the loudest.

Fairy Mask

You will need

Cardboard, thin elastic, pens, pencils, scissors, glitter, glitter pens, scraps of material, glue.

Draw the basic shape of your mask on to the cardboard. Draw some holes where you'll be able to see through and a ridge to go over your nose. Also, mark a hole either side to attach your elastic through.

Draw the fairies which will be stuck to the side of the mask. We folded the card in half and drew ours on one side. Trace ours if you like.

Cut around the mask and fairies and begin to think about how to decorate them.

We made a little Tutu for each fairy and glued it on, but you could paint one on. We made wool hair with sparkles on it too. Paint the mask and decorate it with glitter and pretty things – petals, feathers, confetti and so on.

Thread the elastic through the holes, and try it on for size. Pull the elastic tight and knot it either side. Now remove it.

Glue on your fairies and try the whole mask on.

Did you know?

Fairies are famous for playing little fairy pranks – they never mean any harm but they do enjoy being naughty. There are some things you can do to protect yourself from little fairy pranks. You can turn your clothes inside out, ring bells, put a cross on top of your cakes to stop fairies dancing on them, wear a daisy chain, put a sock under your pillow, have a horseshoe or wear a red thread on your clothes or in you hair.

Hundreds of fairies work and play in every garden but you can only see them if you believe in them. It's said that finding a four-leaf clover can help you see fairies.

Fairy Days
Lady Day – 25th March
Walpurgis Night – 30 th April
MayDay – 30th April
Midsummer's Eve and Day 23rd and 24th June
Christmas Eve and Day 24th and 25th December

Other Ideas

We are making a fairy mask, but there are tons of different masks you could make:

*

Bunnies

*

Flowers

*

Monsters

*

Butterflies

*

Tigers

*

Monkeys

*

91

mmm... Melty Ice-cream Sandwich

What to do

These are real treats. The secret is to make a really light sponge cake to use for the "sandwich bread", so when it's frozen, it is still soft to eat.

Turn the oven on at 180°C or gas 5.

Begin by whisking the eggs and the sugar together until they are very light and frothy. Slowly dribble in the melted butter and keep whisking. The final stage is to sift the flour on top of the egg fluff and then fold it in to try to keep as much air in as possible.

Pour this mixture on to the cake tin, lined with the baking paper and put it in the oven for about 11 or 12 minutes. The cake will go golden on top, and be quite springy when you push the centre with your finger.

Take it out of the oven and leave it to cool on a cooling rack. Peel off the paper and cut the cake in half. Take the ice cream out of the freezer to let it soften up. When the sponge is totally cold, take the tub of ice cream and spread it over one half of the sponge. Then put the other half of sponge on the top. Freeze the whole big slab of sandwich until the ice cream has gone hard again, and you are ready to start to cut your sandwiches. Wrap them in a little piece of baking paper to help catch the ice ceam drips and start eating!

Ingredients

5 eggs
150g caster sugar
70g melted butter
150g plain flour
1 swiss roll tin
baking parchment
1 tub of your favourite ice cream

Bona munching a fast melting sandwich

Make your own healthier option – try blending frozen fruit with honey and natural yoghurt.

Did you know, the biggest ice-cream sundae was 12ft tall and made with 4,667 gallons of ice cream?

July
Facts & Legends

Henley royal regatta. This takes place during the first week of July on a stretch of the river Thames at Henley on Thames in Oxfordshire. The regatta began in 1839 with a single afternoon of rowing races and now lasts for five days.

St Margaret's Day

July 20th. St Margaret was once a very popular patron saint of childbirth. She had the nickname of St Peg. People believed that honouring Peg would bring them Gods protection against illness and evil spirits. St Peg's Day was traditionally celebrated with a plum pudding called Heg Peg Dump.

Whitstable oyster festival is held on the 25th, marking the start of the oyster season. It is said, never eat an oyster in any month with an 'R' in it. The 1st Thursday after the 25th is the day the boats are blessed on St Reeves beach.

Vintners procession, is when the wine merchants of London, march through the city. At the front of the march, 2 men in smocks and top hats, sweep the streets to brush away dung and dirt, so the vintners don't slip or trip.

St James's Day

This day is also known as grotto day. Children used to make grottoes and caves and decorate them with seashells because the scallop shell is supposed to be the emblem of St James. The grottoes were placed outside the homes and the children would sit down by them and say: please remember the grotto. It's only once a year. Father's gone to sea, Mothers gone to bring him back, So please remember me.

St Swithin's Day Legend says if it rains on St Swithin's Day it will carry on for 40 days. This story began in 971, when St Swithin's bones were moved to Winchester Cathedral. There was a huge storm that lasted for 40 days and people said it was the saint weeping in heaven for his moved bones.

Swan Upping

Two of the oldest London guilds, the wine merchants and the dyers, take to their boats to try to catch the swans on the Thames. All the swans on the river belong to the Queen, except for those marked on their beaks, which belong to the dyers and vintners. Upping means turning the birds upside down, to establish ownership of the cygnets by inspecting their parents. After swan upping, the dyers and vintners settle down to a banquet of roast swan. The custom dates back to the 14th century.

Crop Circles

July is the month when circular flattened patches begin to appear in fields of standing corn.

It all began in the 1970s although they had been seen before that. Some experts believe it could be wind or bacteria in the soil, but other people think we may have been visited by beings in crafts from outer space.

August

Lammas Day

In English-speaking countries, 1 August is Lammas Day
(loaf-mass day), the festival of the first wheat harvest
of the year. On this day it was customary
to bring to church a loaf made from the new crop.

The Anglo-Saxon's referred to it as "the feast of
the firstfruits".

8th month

August's flower is the Gladiolus | August's gemstone is the Agate | August is named after the Roman Emperor Augustus

MON	TUES	WED	THURS	FRI	SAT	SUN
				📖 Lammas Day (Christian) Total solar eclipse **1**	**2**	Columbus set sail on 1st voyage 1492 **3**
Bank Holiday Scotland 📖 Britain went to war in 1914 **4**	**5**	📖 The Sandwich invented. Named after 'The Earl of Sandwich' 1762 **6**	**7**	📖 Great train robbery (1963) **8**	**9**	Tishah B'AV (Jewish) **10**
The Glorious 12th (grouse season begins) Perseid meteor shower **11**	International Left hander's Day **12**	**13**	**14**	Corporal punishment in schools banned 1987 **15**	Partial lunar eclipse National Joke Day **16**	**17**
Helium Discovered on the Sun 1868 **18**	**19**	**20**	Tooth Fairy Day (USA) **21**	**22**	Mount Vesuvius erupted near Pompeii (Italy) 79AD 📖 Notting Hill Carnival **24**	**23**
Summer Bank Holiday 📖 Notting Hill Carnival **25**	Romans landed in Britain 55BC **26**	📖 Martin Luther King speech 1963 (Washington) **27**	**28**	**29**	**30**	Princess Diana. Died 1997 **31**

Leo 24th July – 23rd August

Virgo 24th August – 23rd September

Hi Jago

   We are back from the States, but we left on the day before tooth fairy day. Mum said she would take me to Notting Hill carnival instead to cheer me up and we have some old tins in the garden which we are turning into drums — Jah man!

   Polly XX

Jago Harris

204 Latimer Road

London W10 6QY

Hi Polly

We are all going to Cornwall for two weeks Dad says he will take me out in the boat to catch mackerel and put out lobster pots we have a favourite game that we play on the beach called pebble pants too. Next year you should come and stay it would be really fun.

   Lol Jago

Polly Loughney

Honeysuckle Cottage

Lower Baldridge
Oxon OX8 4PT

Floating Koi Carps

Other Ideas

Why don't you try?

*

Stars – the streamers could be asteroids

*

Try faces – and tie the streamers into bunches

1 Draw an outline of a fish on the piece of card and cut it out. Then trace around it and cut out that piece too. They can be as big or small as you like. Begin to decorate the fish, but make sure you check which side to do. You are eventually going to glue the two together.

2 We use felt brush tip pens, but our trick is to shade in the areas and then, with wet fingers, rub the pen marks and they start to bleed into one another and make it look like paints. You can decorate these how you like. You could cut discs from old colourful magazines and stick them to your fish like scales, or use even more glitter than we did. It's up to you.

3 Once you have decorated the outsides of your fish, tear the tissue into long strips to make the tail. These need to be stuck to the undecorated side of the fish's tail with your glue. Once they are in position, sandwich both sides together using plenty of glue so they don't come undone.

4 Make a hole near the fish's mouth and thread through the string, and it's ready to use. Try to hang these from the ceiling somewhere it's breezy so the tail can really flutter, and it's really good if you get the chance to make even more and hang them all up together.

This is a really pretty thing to make, especially if there is a baby in your house. They love these even more than we do.

You will need

Stiff card, felt brush tip pens, glue, tissue paper, sparkles and glitters, string.

Bright and Beautiful BBQ

What to do

Begin by lighting the barbeque and get the charcoals hot and ready for action. In the meantime, cut the sweet potatoes in half and skin side down put them on the bbq to start their cooking. They take some time to soften in the middle so begin cooking them as soon as the bbq has some heat to it. Put the chicken in a bowl and sprinkle the jerk spice mix on top and rub it into the chicken so it coats all of the meat. Leave this in the fridge until the bbq is ready. It gives the chicken a chance to marinate.

Heat the butter in a bowl or food processor and add the grated zest of the limes and the red chillis chopped as small as you can. Be careful that you don't rub your eyes with your chilli fingers! Ouch. Now you've made a yummy chilli butter to rub on your corn on the cobs. The bbq should be hot now. Take the corn on the cobs and the chicken and place it on the bbq rack with the sweet potatoes. It's going to take a while to cook all the way through. Add a little oil to the chicken to help it sizzle in and remember to keep turning all these delicious things over with tongs so they don't go too black on one side. After about half an hour, cut the chicken with a knife and make sure the juices coming out of it are running clear and not pinky red. It's done when it's clear. Squeeze lemon juice and lime juice over it to make your mouth water even more and get munching. Rub butter all over your corn on the cob and let it melt and you can mop your sweet potato up too.

Ingredients

- 2 sweet potatoes
- 4 corn on the cobs
- 4 chicken legs
- 4 chicken breasts
- jerk spice
- vegetable oil
- 100g butter
- 2 red chillis
- 1 lime
- 1 lemon
- salt and pepper
- a barbeque
- charcoal

Barbeque may be from the french barbe à queue (from whiskers to tail).

Why don't you try something sweet on the bbq like bananas or fruit skewers.

Polly - Papa's Garden, August

Papier Mâché Volcano

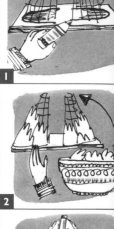

You will need

A board about 2x2 feet, chicken wire, lots of old newspaper, wallpaper paste, paints, 1 large sheet of paper, sticky tape, 20cm piece of hosepipe or similar, baking soda, vinegar red food colouring, 1 balloon.

Begin by making the chicken wire bend into 2 halves of a volcano shape (a cone but cut in half). Sit these on the board and draw around the edge of them. Take them off the board and mix up the wallpaper paste.

Start to shred the old papers and dip them into the glue. Stick them over the shell that is going to make the volcano, and leave them to dry a bit before putting on the next layer. Keep going until you have a smooth but textured covering all over it. Let this go hard and dry.

In the middle of one of the sides, attach the piece of hose with sticky tape and push both pieces of the volcano together. It sounds a bit complicated; look at our diagram. Then the fun begins.

Decorate the outside of the volcano with the paints. Remember it was covered with lava once! I have put in a cross section of a volcano inside mine. Look at the picture below.

When everything is painted and decorated, you can put some of the baking soda and vinegar in the balloon, attach the balloon to the bottom of the hose, push the volcano back together, mix some red colouring with water and pour it down the hose.

Stand back! Your pretend molten lava is about to explode from the top crater and run down the side.

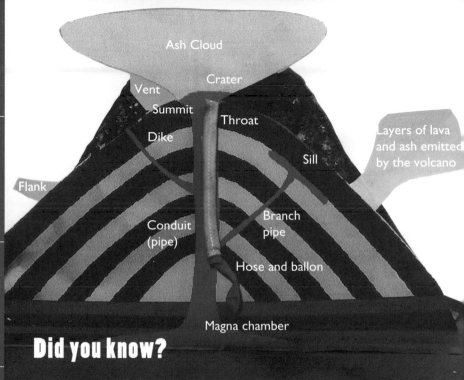

Ash Cloud

Crater

Vent

Summit

Throat

Dike

Sill

Flank

Layers of lava and ash emitted by the volcano

Conduit (pipe)

Branch pipe

Hose and ballon

Magna chamber

Did you know?

Italy has a lot of volcanic history. Famously Vesuvius erupted in 79AD and destroyed the 2 Roman cities called Pompeii and Herculaneum.

A volcano is the name given to the conical mountain left after the vent has been used by the molten lava that bubbles in the core of the earth's crust and forces its way out or erupts, showering lava, ash and rock everywhere.

The lava is so hot it burns everything in its way. That includes houses, people, wildlife and plant life.

There are more than 500 active volcanoes in the world, and no one can really tell when the next eruption will happen.

There are 4 types of volcano: active, intermittent, dormant and extinct.

We use part of a volcano in the form of pumice stone. It is really good at rubbing hard skin off feet.

The word volcano probably comes from the Roman god of fire, Vulcan.

Although ash is harmful to begin with, it will eventually turn into very fertile soil.

Yummy Summer Pudding

What to do

Place all the berries in a pan with 50ml of water and bring them up to the boil. Let the berries begin to swell and pop a little to release their beautiful juices. Taste this juice and add as much sugar as you need to make it sweet enough. Cut the crusts off the bread and cut them in half. Dip one side of the bread in the fruit's juices and pack it into the pudding basin. See our picture.

Keep doing this until the whole bowl is covered in sticky purple bread. Tip some of the fruit into the bread bowl and put another piece of bread on top of that. Then repeat the process and finish the top off with bread. Wrap this with cling film, put a plate on top a little smaller than the bowl and put something very heavy on top of the plate. The pressure makes all the berry juice soak into the bread making it purple. Leave this pud in the fridge for 24 to 48 hours and then get ready to tip it out on to a plate ready to serve. Ease the bread around the edge with a knife to loosen it and then shake the basin. It should gently flop out on to your plate. It's really yummy with ice cream.

Ingredients

1 loaf of thinly sliced white bread
500g mixed summer berries
(or a bag of frozen fruits)
sugar to taste
1 large pudding basin

Bruce's birthday surprise – didn't last long with all of us around!

Did you know eating a big blueberry is as good as eating a big vitamin tablet?

Did you know that you can freeze berries really successfully? They're really delicious with a hot white chocolate sauce!

August
Facts & Legends

Great Train Robbery
On the 8th of August, gold bullion was stolen from a Royal Mail train. The robbers all emigrated from England. Police have spent years tracking them down.

The Earl of Sandwich
The Earl of Sandwich was playing cards and gambling one night, but instead of interrupting the game to eat their dinner of meat and vegetables, he asked for the meat to be served between two slices of bread. It's possible the sandwich was invented around 1762.

The Great War
On the 4th of August 1914 Britain went to war. It lasted 4 long years. Britain's main enemy was Germany. It started because of the invasion of Poland, amongst other things.

Martin Luther King
On 28th August 1963 an American human rights activist gave a speech beginning with "I have a dream..." He fought to get equal rights for black people.

August
August is one of the busiest months for wildlife. The birds are already planning to fly south to avoid the cold.

Insects and bugs are much noisier this month than any other, and they all breed this month too.

Notting Hill Carnival
is a colourful procession of floats and dancers. It started when West Indian and Caribbean families celebrated their cultural traditions from home.

Rush Bearing

In the middle ages before carpets were used, people used to put rushes on their floors.

Many villages held a special summer ceremony when the rushes were harvested. In some villages, people used to make rush sculptures, called "Bearings".

They were carried around in a procession. In parts of north-west England and Cumbria, people still follow this ancient custom.

Lammas Day

Lammas Day is known for lots of reasons. Many traditions and customs stem from this day. It is a time to give thanks for the harvest that's about to begin. Lammas Day was celebrated by pagans way before the Christian harvest festival in this country was started. Harvest festivals are celebrated by most faiths and religions, by way of thanking God for crops and prosperity.

Lammas day used to be a time for "trial marriages" lasting for about 11 days, to see if the marriage would work. If it didn't work, the couple would separate. In Exeter, farmers used to give their workers a pair of leather gloves. Farmers in some areas would let the first corn bread go stale and then crumble it over the corners of their barns for luck in the future.

September

Thirty Days Hath September – Aide Memoire!

Thirty days hath September,
April, June and November,
February has twenty-eight alone,
All the rest have thirty-one.

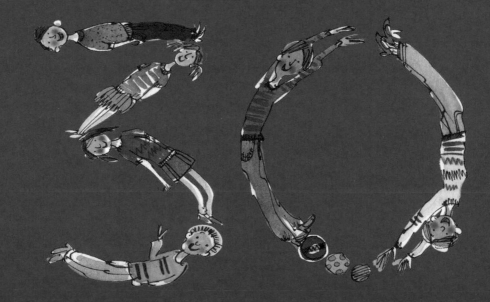

9th month

September's flower is the Aster

September's gemstone is the Sapphire

September originally meant the seventh month and was guarded by Vulcan, God of fire

MON	TUES	WED	THURS	FRI	SAT	SUN
Asteroid 3, Juno Discovered 1804 **1**	Ramadan starts (Islam) Great fire of London 1666 **2**	Ganesh Chaturthi (Indian festival) **3**	**4**	**5**	**6**	**7**
Magellan set sail for 1st voyage around the world 1519 **8**	William the conquerour died 1087 **9**	**10**	**11**	**12**	Roald Dahl, author. Born 1916 **13**	Holy Cross Day (Christian) **14**
15	International Day of Peace **16**	**17**	George Cadbury, Cadbury chocolates. Born 1839 **18**	**19**	International Student Day **20**	World Gratitude Day **21**
1st Day of Autum Elephant Appreciation Day **22**	Harvest officialy begins Jim Henson, muppeteer. Born 1936. **23**	**24**	**25**	TS Eliot, poet. Born 1888 **26**	**27**	St Wenceslas Day **28**
Michaelmas Day **29**	Rosh Hashanah (Jewish) **30**					

Virgo 24th August – 23rd September

Libra 24th September – 24th October

Hi Jago

How are you, hope Cornwall was
fab. Jamila's mum has invited me
to go to their house for eid al fitr
which marks the end of Ramadan
I'm really excited it's a massive
feast day in their house.

Polly XX

Jago Harris

20u Latimer Road

London W10 6QY

Hi Polly

Me and some friends from school
decorated the church today for
harvest festival and everybody
brought in some food from home
Jim brought beans while Jemima
brought in the biggest marrow
anyone had ever seen strange

from Jago

Polly Loughney

Honeysuckle Cottage

Lower Baldridge
Oxon OX8 4PT

Leaf Rubbing

1 At any time of year there are lovely shaped leaves to choose from. Pick a couple. We used horsechestnut leaves. Put them on the table. Place your paper over the top and rub over the leaves with the crayons. You can be quite autumnal with the colours, or psychedelic if you like, there are no rules about the colours.

2 Once you have made a good collection of different leaf rubbings, you can cut around their outline and make a collage with them. It's good fun to learn about the shapes of different trees' leaves and to try to recognise them outside. Draw outlines of the different trees' we see every day and the seeds, for example conkers or sycamore helicopter seeds.

Other Ideas

Why don't you try?

*

Other shaped leaves

*

Charcoal

*

Different coloured paper

*

Rubbing other things with texture (bricks, wood, engravings)

You will need

Leaves, crayons, paper, scissors.

Wild Mushroom Risotto

Start preparing the mushrooms, make sure there are no bits of forest trying to hide in the ridges or gills of them and trim the woody dried end away too. Melt the butter in a large saucepan. Add the chopped onion and garlic and let them go golden brown. When you get to this stage, add the wild mushrooms and sauté them. Next, in goes the Arborio rice, stir to make sure the butter has coated all of the grains. Turn the heat down on the stove top for a few minutes and add the first 100ml of vegetable stock. Keep stirring so nothing sticks to the bottom of the pan. Slowly add the stock in 100ml batches until the rice has absorbed all the liquid and has become soft. Stir in the handful of fresh parsley and spoon the mixture on to a plate or a bowl, then drizzle the oil over the top if you are using it, and grate some parmesan over the top too.

Ingredients

200g Arborio risotto rice
400g mixed wild mushrooms.
(we used 4 varieties)
50g butter
1 onion
2 cloves of garlic
salt and papper
1 handful of flat leaf parsley
500ml vegetable stock
parmesan
olive oil or truffle oil (optional)

Did you know the brighter the mushroom the more deadly they can be – think of the red toadstools.

Grandma's birthday supper

There are loads of different varieties of rice – basmati, pudding, sushi, wild... Can you think of any more?

Hedgehog Bread Rolls

You will need

500g strong white bread flour,
and a bit extra to flour your surface
7g sachet of dried yeast
or 15g fresh yeast
1 tablespoon of salt
300ml lukewarm water
1 tablespoon of butter
a handful of currants
1 teaspoon of sugar
1 baking sheet
baking paper
scissors
dress pins for eyes

Did you know?

The idea of making
bread is to make it as
airy as possible. Yeast
likes warmth, so keep
everything you're working
with warm where possible.

Begin by activating the yeast. You need to crumble or sprinkle it into 200ml of the lukewarm water with the sugar and leave it to bubble on the surface for a short while. Meanwhile, sift the flour into a bowl and stir in the salt.

Put the flour and salt into a bowl. Make a well in the middle and pour in the yeast water into it. Bring the flour in from around the edges using your hands. Keep mixing from the edge in. When you have a lumpy-looking mess in your bowl, tip it on to a floured work-bench and start to knead it.

After about 10 minutes the dough will become really smooth and ready to start work. Put it back in the bowl and put a damp cloth over the top. The yeast will start rising in the dough and when it's doubled in size you are ready for the next stage. Be really rough with it, and slap all of the air out of it.

Then knead it again and cut it into 16 even-sized pieces, and start to shape it into teardrop shapes. Take a pair of scissors and snip into the dough to make some spikes for the hedgehog. Press 2 currants in the sharp end of the dough tears to make hedgehog eyes.

Put the dough hogs on the buttered baking sheet and leave them to rise up again. When they are nearly joined together, they must go into the oven. Brush them with a little milk first and then bake them until they are really golden and crusty.

The oven needs to be 220 °C or gas mark 7 to bake these beauties and they take about 15 to 20 minutes to cook. Let them cool on a rack and they are ready either to eat or to make your harvest festival display.

Did you know?

Some animals have to decide whether to hibernate, migrate or adapt for winter. For some small animals it's a necessity to hibernate for survival. A small animal burns up fat from the food it eats faster than larger creatures, and the fact food is harder to find, means in winter, hibernation is their best option

Animals that hibernate, usually find themselves a cosy den, burrow or hollow log for shelter and protection. Their body temperatures drop and their rate of breathing is much slower. When they go into true hibernation, they are almost impossible to wake up. Most animals will eat masses of food, bulking up their body fat so they can nourish themselves through winter.

Some animals don't go into a completely deep sleep, but a sort of dormant state when their heart beats really slow down, but their temperature is still really high. You can still manage to wake them up, although they'd probably be a bit grumpy about it. This dormant state leaves the creature with enough energy to see the winter through.

Some animals that hibernate are;

Badgers, bears, bats, butterflies and moths, although some migrate, frogs, chipmunks, groundhogs, hamsters, hedgehogs, ladybirds mice, raccoons, rodents, squirrels and turtles.

Migration can often be the best option for some creatures, it means they travel to warmer places where they can find food and survive the winter.

Some frogs and other reptiles live at the bottom of ponds and lakes during hibernation. It's warmer for them and they can absorb more oxygen through cold water than warm water.

You can help small animals through the winter by feeding them things like peanuts, seeds and dried fruits. You could even make a feeder by smearing a fir cone with peanut butter and hanging from a tree.

Hedgerow Apple and Blackberry Crumble

What to do

Preheat your oven to 425°C or gas mark 7.
Peel the apples and slice them thinly. Rinse the blackberries and put them into the same bowl as the slices of apple. Sprinkle the cinnamon on if you'd like to use it. Sift the flour into a bowl and add the butter in little lumps. Rub the butter and the flour through your fingertips until it looks like breadcrumbs, stir in the sugar and mix it well. There are other things you can add to the crumble topping. For example, oats, spices, dried fruits, muesli, or if you are making a savoury crumble you can add herbs or cheese. Put the fruit into a saucepan with about 50ml of water and let it soften slightly for a few minutes. Sweeten it if you like and then tip it into the ovenproof dish. Sprinkle the flour mixture over the top and put the dish in the oven. A crumble takes about 20 minutes, but as soon as it's golden on top, it's ready to come out of the oven. Let it cool a bit before you eat it.

Ingredients

500g cooking apples
500g blackberries
225g butter
225g plain flour
200g golden caster sugar
cinnamon if you like it
1 oven-proof dish

We picked the blackberries for this from the hedgerow ourselves!

Savoury crumbles can be really yummy too – why don't you try cheesy leeks or mince and tomatoes are nice.

Why don't you try adding oats or cinnamon, raisins or chocolate flakes to your crumble mixture.

September
Facts & Legends

Conkers

No one quite knows where or why the game of conkers originated, but children have been playing it for centuries. There are lots of different ways to make your conker the best.

Two of our tips are to soak it in vinegar for 2 days, then dry it out in the airing cupboard for another 2 days. See if it works for you too!

Michaelmas

It's a very old superstition that when Archangel Michael kicked the devil out of heaven, he fell to earth and landed on a bramble bush.

He kicked it, cursed it and spat at it with his fiery breath, so it has been a tradition that it's a bad idea to pick and eat blackberries after the Michaelmas holiday.

Great Fire of London

On the 2nd of September 1666, a fire began in a bakery off Pudding Lane in London. It burned for at least 4 days, destroyed 89 churches, 13,200 houses and 430 streets. Only 6 people died in the fire.

The Gregorian Calendar

In 1752, the British Empire adopted the Gregorian calendar. It was named after Pope Gregory VIII who introduced it in 1582, and it is based around the movement of the stars and moon.

Ramadan begins in the 9th month of the muslim lunar calendar. Its a month of fasting during daylight hours. Allah ordered it in the Qur'an. It commemorates Archangel Gabriel giving the Qur'an to Muhammad. It's a time of deep thought.

Sir Francis Drake On September 26th 1580, one of England's greatest explorers returned to the port of Plymouth on the **Golden Hind** ship. He was the 1st British navigator to sail around the earth and was rewarded by Elizabeth I.

Corn Dollies

The tradition of making corn dollies dates back hundreds of years. People used to believe there was a goddess who lived in the corn and would die unless some of the corn was saved, so a corn dolly was made to make sure the corn goddess would stay alive for the next harvest. The dolly was made from the last sheaf of wheat.

The Horn Dance

It is thought to be one of the oldest surviving ceremonies in the country. One of the first mentionings of this dance is at the Barthelmy Fair in August 1226. Antlers are used in the dance. Today the ceremony takes place on Wakes Monday. After collecting the horns from the church at 8 in the morning, the dancers dance and play music for about 10 miles in villages and surrounding countryside.

Michaelmas Day

The 29th September is the feast day for the Archangel Michael. St Michael is the patron saint of the sea, ships, boatmen, horses and horsemen, and of knights and grocers.

Michael was best known for his fight with the devil, and how he cast Lucifer out of heaven with all the other angels and is mentioned in the bible, as his band of angels who fought the dragon. Michaelmas Day was traditionally the last day of the harvest season which was also known as Lammas, which means loaf mass. The farmers made bread and took it to the church. Michaelmas Day is often known as goose day too, because geese were taken to fair to sell on this day.

October

It's Punky Night Tonight!

It's Punky Night tonight,
It's Punky Night tonight,
Give us a candle, give us a light,
It's Punky Night tonight!
It's Punky Night tonight,
It's Punky Night tonight,
Adam and Eve won't believe,
It's Punky Night tonight!

It's Punky Night tonight,
It's Punky Night tonight,
Eee-ie, diddley-die,
It's Punky Night tonight!

10th month

VIII

October's flower is the Calendula

October's gemstone is the Opal

October originally meant the eighth month
Bacchus god of wine represented the month of harvest

MON	TUES	WED	THURS	FRI	SAT	SUN
		Chinese National Day / 1st Model T Ford was introduced 1908 **1**	Eid Al Fitr Ramadam Ends (Islam) / Mohandas Gandhi, Leader of India. Born 1869 **2**	SOS Began as international distress in 1906 **3**	St Francis Day / World Animal Day **4**	World Teachers' Day / Poetry Day **5**
World Smile Day / World Space Week **6**	Far side moon 1st observed by Luna 3 in 1959 **7**	**8**	World Post Day / Yom Kippur (Jewish) / Dasera (Hindu) **9**	**10**	Apollo 7 launched from Cape Kennedy 1968 **11**	Columbus Day (USA) / 1st Morris Minor built 1884 (Oxford) **12**
St Edward's Day / Greenwich mean time started 1884 **13**	Battle of Hastings Began 1066 / Sukkot (Jewish) **14**	**15**	World Food Day / Oscar Wilde, author. Born 1854 **16**	St Luke's Day **17**	**18**	**19**
1st message sent between two computers 1966 / Sir Christopher Wren. Born 1632 **20**	Apple Day (Kent) / Battle of Trafalgar 1805 **21**	Simhat Torah (Jewish) **22**	United Nations Day **23**	**24**	St Crispin's Day Patron Saint of shoemakers / Pablo Picasso. Born 1881 **25**	British summer time ends (clocks back one hour) **26**
International School Library Day / Captain James Cook. Born 1728 **27**	Feast of St Jude / Make a Difference Day **28**	**29**	**30**	Halloween **31**		

Scorpio 24th October – 22nd November

Libra 24th September – 23rd October

Hi Jago

It's Halloween today — after school we are dressing up to go trick or treating. My costume is a black cat and my brother Tom is going as a skeleton — if we are lucky we might get some treats home for apple bobbing and eating jaffa cakes off the string yippee.

love Polly

Jago Harris

204 Latimer Road

London W10 6QY

Hi Polly

I have been out in the park near my school collecting up all these amazing conkers some are massive and some are really shiny dad's going to help me stick a skewer through them later so we can tie them onto string and start swinging them — look out knuckles xxJago

Polly Loughney

Honeysuckle Cottage

Lower Baldridge
Oxon OX8 4PT

Pumpkin Carving

1 Start off with a drawing on the pumpkin of what you'd like your pumpkin to look like. Mark has drawn a few scary and funny faces to help, if you get stuck. Once you have drawn on his face, ask the grown up to start cutting the top of the pumpkin off. When there is a " lid", lift it off and start to scoop out all the seeds; you can keep these and make something else with them. Then begin cutting out the face.

2 Put a candle in the bottom of the pumpkin and then put his lid back on. We think they look really good in the window or outside the front door. Don't make them too scary, though.

You will need

Pumpkins that look as though they would make a good face shape once carved, a sharp knife, 1 marker pen, tea light candles, definitely a grown-up to help with the carving.

Scary Pumpkin Soup

What to do

Put the oil in a heavy-based saucepan and add the chopped garlic and onion. Stir this in the oil until it begins to go golden brown.

Add the chunks of pumpkin, we added chopped red chilli and some of the stalks from the fresh coriander. Leave the leaves for decoration. Let all of the ingredients become coated with oil and begin browning. When the chilli is softened and the pumpkin is getting a bit raggedy around the edges, pour in the vegetable stock and bring the mixture up to the boil.

Put a lid on if you have one. It makes it all happen a little bit quicker. The pumpkin needs to soften in the liquid. When that happens you are ready to whisk the soup. If you have an electric blender, use that, otherwise, mash it with a potato masher and push it all through a sieve. This gets rid of any lumps. Add some salt and pepper and pour some soup into either a cup or bowl. Decorate the top with a few rings of chilli and some of the left-over coriander leaves.

We serve ours with cheese straws, but you could serve it with bread, croutons or bread sticks.

Ingredients

half a pumpkin, peeled and cut into chunks
2 chopped onions
2 cloves of garlic
2 red chillis
1 small bunch of coriander
1 litre of vegetable stock
60ml vegetable or olive oil

Tea before trick or treating

If you make cheese straws, why don't you try cutting them out like hearts or stars.

Orange foods contain the most vitamin C. it's known as happy food.

Skeleton Costume

You will need

Black tights or leggings, black t-shirt, black gloves, iron-on white backing fabric, an iron, a photocopied enlargement of our bones.

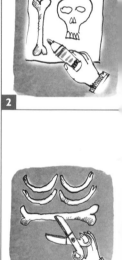

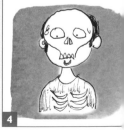

Photocopy the picture of the bones we have got on this page. Enlarge them, probably about 250% bigger, but it does depend how big the costume is going to be. Trace around the edge of the big bones you'd like to use, on to the white backing fabric. We only used about 12, but you can go crazy and use the lot. If you like bones, you might like to write the name of each bone on your outfit.

You are ready to cut the bones out now. Remember where they are on the body for the next stage. Take your black leggings and t-shirt and pin the bones into position.

Ask a grown-up to iron these on to the black clothes. Next thing to do is take all the pins out and try on your outfit. To make it really scary, try making a skull mask using the outline we have given you.

You could trace it on to white card and cut it out. Then thread some elastic through either side and wear it over your face.

DON'T BE TOO SCARY THOUGH!!!

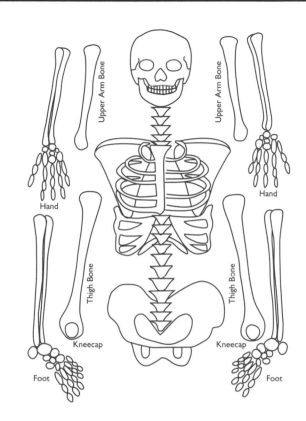

Did you know?

Did you know that human grown-ups have around 206 bones, 100 of them in our hands and feet alone? Babies have about 300 when they are born but as they grow many separate bones fuse together to form single bones – think of your skull, for example.

Bones make our blood and protect us. In our bones we have marrow. This is where we make millions of new blood cells every day, which are circulated all around our body. Bones are a bit like armour for our organs really – without the bones in our skull the brain wouldn't have any protection, the same with our heart and lungs, which are behind our ribcage.

It's really important to get lots of calcium (a mineral) as this is what our bones are mostly made up of – this is found in milk and other dairy products like cheese and ice cream. There is also a good deal of calcium in green leafy vegetables like spinach.

Funny Runny Honey Comb and Crunchy Toffee Apples

What to do

For the honeycomb

Place a heavy-based saucepan on the stove hob. In it put the syrup and the sugar and let it all dissolve and bubble up together. When it starts to bubble and the sugar has melted, add the bicarbonate of soda. Stir it well and when it begins to expand, pour it on-to a baking tray lined with silicone paper. Leave it to cool in the fridge and when it does, smash it up into pieces.

For the toffee apples

Place the sugar in a heavy-based saucepan and put it on the stove top on a medium-high heat to start the caramel. While this starts to go brown around the edge of the pan, wash and dry the apples and then stick a chopstick in one end of each. Give the caramel a wiggle in the pan to stop any areas going too dark, and when all the sugar has dissolved, you can start to dunk your apples. BE REALLY CAREFUL. IT WILL BURN YOU VERY BADLY IF YOU SPLASH IT ON YOUR SKIN. Use a spoon if you like to help coat the apples, and when you have an even coat of caramel, stand the apple on some of the silicone paper. Scatter some hundreds and thousands on them now before the caramel sets.

When it's cold they are ready to eat. A tip to get the pan clean afterwards is to fill it with water and boil it on the stove.

Ingredients

For the honeycomb

75g of caster sugar
30ml of golden syrup
30g bicarbonate of soda
1 baking tray
silicone paper

For the toffee apples

4 eating apples
2 pairs of wooden chopsticks
250g caster sugar
sugar strands or hundreds and thousands
silicone paper

You can try coating your honeycomb in chocolate if you like and make your own crunchie bars.

Try slicing apples really thinly then popping them in the oven at gas mark 0.5 till they are crisp - yummy!

We suddenly became really popular with all of these!

October
Facts & Legends

The Battle of Hastings
was on 14th October 1066. King Harold was defeated by William of Normandy. King Harold was killed by an arrow being shot in his eye. William became known as William the Conqueror and proclaimed king of England.

St Francis Day
On 4th of October, St Francis Day, swallows are meant to fly to the bottom of the ponds and hibernate through the winter. Many years ago this seemed the best explanation for their sudden disappearance.

St Francis of Assisi was a very wealthy young man who had wasted his money on naughty behaviour and wild living, but he saw a vision of Jesus and became really pious. He died on the 4th of October 1226 and the day was named after him.

Captain James Cook
On the 6th October 1769, Captain James Cook discovered New Zealand. His ship was called the *Explorer*. A replica was made in the late 1990s and sailed around the world as a tribute to him and his crew.

Apollo 7 was launched from Cape Kennedy in America on 11th October 1968. It made its first manned flight in the command module which was the forerunner of the mission that carried men to the moon.

Mop Fairs
Servants and farm labourers would work from October to October and then go to the centre of the village to hire themselves out for the next year to come.

They wore their best clothes and to let people know what kind of work they wanted. A maid would carry a mop, a shepherd had wool, a gardener had flowers and so on. Once they had been chosen the master would take off their sign and put on some bright ribbons.

Halloween or Eve of All Hallows is on 31st October. It has its beginnings in the old Celtic feast of Samhain which marked the final day of the Celtic year. Originally it was called the festival of the dead when people chased away evil spirits.

Edward the Confessor's Day

A special service commemorates the last Anglo-Saxon King of England and the founder of Westminster Abbey. He was known as the Confessor because of his monk-like generosity to the poor. He was also married to a woman called Edith but they never consummated their marriage. One story that has become a famous legend is when Edward was riding by a church in Essex and an old man asked for money.

Edward didn't have any, but he gave the man one of his large rings from his finger. A few years later two pilgrims travelling in the Holy Land became stranded. They were helped by an old man who, when he found out they came from England, told them he was St John the Evangelist and asked them to give the ring back to Edward and to tell him he would be joining him in heaven within 6 months.

Pumpkin Night

This is the last Thursday of October. The tradition goes back over 100 years, when it's thought that the men from Hinton travelled to a fair at Chiselborough, Somerset.

When they didn't come back as they said, the women went to look for their husbands using mangold lanterns. A mangold is a type of crop grown to feed cattle. It looks a bit like a pumpkin and a turnip. They carved the vegetable and put a candle inside and then went in search of their drunken husbands. Nowadays on Punky Night, local children join the procession singing Punky Night songs, swinging their lanterns and sometimes getting a few pennies from people at their doors. It is a bit like trick and treating.

November

Remember, Remember

Remember, remember the fifth of November,
The gunpowder, treason, and plot,
I know of no reason why the gunpowder treason
Should ever be forgot.
Guy Fawkes, Guy Fawkes, 'twas his intent
To blow up the King and Parliament.
Three score barrels of powder below,
Poor old England to overthrow;
By God's providence he was catch'd
With a dark lantern and burning match.
Holloa boys, holloa boys, make the bells ring.
Holloa boys, holloa boys, God save the King!
Hip hip hoorah!

11th month

November's flower is the Chrysanthemum

November's gemstone is the Topaz

November originally meant the ninth month and was represented by Pluto, god of the underworld

MON	TUES	WED	THURS	FRI	SAT	SUN
					All Saints' Day (Christian) Day of the Dead (Mexico) **1**	All Souls' Day (Christian) **2**
3	Mischief Night **4**	Guy Fawkes Night **5**	**6**	Marie Curie. Born 1867 **7**	Lord Major's Show. London **8**	Remembrance Sunday 1st giant panda collected alive in China 1927 **9**
Armistice Day (2 minute silence at 11am) Martinmas Day **10**	Auguste Rodin, sculptor. Born 1840 **11 12**	Guru Nanak Dev Sahib (Sikh) **13**	Childen's Day (India) Prince Charles. Born 1948 **14**	**15**	**16**	
17	**18**	Universal Children's Day (UNICEF) Windsor Castle damaged by fire 1992 **19 20**	**21**	St Cecilia's Day **22**	St Clement's Day (Patron St of blacksmiths) Stir Up Sunday **23**	
24	**25**	Thanksgiving (Interfaith USA) **26**	William Blake, poet and artist. Born 1757 **27 28**	**29**	St Andrew's Day Advent Sunday Winston Churchill, Born 1874 **30**	

Scorpio 24th October – 22nd November

Sagittarius 23rd November – 21st December

Hi Jago

Whizz bang pop yikes, my ears
are still ringing from our village
fireworks party last night my
friends and I had made a guy
to go on the top of the fire and
we got to drink loads of hot
chocolate with marshmallows to
keep warm yummy.

from Polly

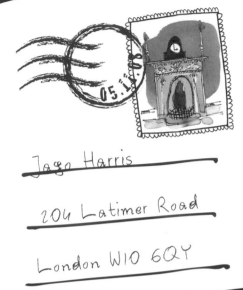

Jago Harris

204 Latimer Road

London W10 6QY

Hi Polly

I'm a bit tired today we had a
pyjama party at our house for
mischief night in the middle of the
night we crept around the house
and put things in the wrong place
it was so funny — Jim put the
remote control in the fridge! Dad
will never find it!

from Jago

Polly Loughney

Honeysuckle Cottage

Lower Baldridge
Oxon OX8 4PT

Fireworks Wax Drawing

1. Begin by colouring in the thick white paper. We drew squares on to the paper and then coloured in each square with a bright colour. The black crayons are needed next to cover all of the coloured squares. Make it as thick as you can, so no colour can be seen through it.

2. The fun begins. Make a design in your head or on a piece of paper of what your picture will look like. Then take your scratcher and scrape off the black crayon, which will leave all the colour on view underneath.

There are lots of different designs your could do.

*

We thought of animals' faces, flowers.

*

Make these into birthday cards and scrape off the crayon, but instead of a picture you can write happy birthday instead.

*

You could use a silver or gold pen on the paper below the crayon and then have a metallic design showing through.

You will need

Thick paper, felt tip pens, black wax crayons, something for scratching; we used a skewer.

Whizz, Bang Pop Spicy Bangers and Boston Beans

What to do

Begin by choosing a heavy-bottomed, big pan. Put the olive oil in it and get it hot. Add the chopped garlic and onions and stir them until they begin to go golden. Add the bacon next and get that sizzling. The next ingredients to go in are the beans and the tomatoes. Bring all of this lovely stuff up to boiling and leave it to simmer for 4 or 5 minutes. Turn the heat down on the pan now and add the treacle and some salt and pepper.

Simmer it again for about 10 to 15 minutes and then take it off the heat. Chop the parsley and stir it through the beans, and meanwhile grill the sausages until they are golden and cooked all the way through. Add the sausages to the beans, give everything a really good stir and you are ready to serve it all up.

Ingredients

1 tin of cannellini beans
1 tin of chopped tinned tomatoes
1 bunch of flat leaf parsley
2 tablespoons of black treacle
100g chopped bacon or pancetta (raw)
1 onion
2 cloves of garlic
50ml olive oil
200ml vegetable stock
8 sausages
salt and pepper

Sausages with Harvey before the fireworks display

Did you know Germany is the biggest sausage eating country in the world.

When you chop up chillies you should wash your hands really well afterwards so it doesn't sting your skin.

Rocket Superstructure

You will need

Thick card, paper, coloured pens, paint, sticky stars, tissue paper, glue, sticky tape, glitter, scissors.

Start by making a cylinder with the thick card. Our design has 2 porthole windows with an astronaut looking out. Then make a stand for the rocket, which is a bit like a launchpad. Slot 2 pieces of the card together to make a cross.

Snip down into one side of each of the rectangle pieces and then they should slide together neatly. Draw or paint the stand. You could draw the launchpad on yours, we drew trees. Stand the cylinder of the rocket on top.

Make a cone for the nose of the rocket, by cutting a semi-circle of card and bending it around until the 2 straight sides meet and then stick it together inside using sticky tape.

Put your design on the nose cone and then dribble glue around the top of the cylinder. Put the nose cone on top of it, and apply just a little pressure for a second, to get rid of any glue bubbles and make sure it's going to stick.

Final touches for our rocket were streamers coming out of the bottom, where the engines are, which look a bit like fire and smoke.

We think it's best if you cover your nose cone with moon dust (glitter), but try to avoid asteroids when flying this rocket!

Did you know?

SPACE FACTS

Our planet earth has one moon, but some planets like Mars have 3 and Saturn has 30! Neil Armstrong was the first man to walk on earth's moon in 1969.

Some people are trying to buy land in outer space.

A nebula is a cloud of dust and gas in outer space. These clouds are often very large, spanning lots of light years. Astronauts have seen these from their spacecrafts and satellites have taken photos of them.

NASA, or the National Aeronautics and Space Administration, uses a shuttle, which is a cross between an aeroplane and a rocket. They do experiments in space to learn more about weightlessness in humans, and experiment with medicines and technology. They set up future space explorations too.

Today only astronauts can visit space, mainly because it is very expensive. But NASA is making spacecraft that will replace the shuttle and make travel cheaper, which may mean we can all afford to take our holidays in space!

Cheeky Chocolate Brownies

What to do

Put the oven on to get hot to gas mark 4 or 180°C, and then line the tray with the paper to stop the brownies sticking to it. Put a pan of water on to boil, and in a bowl put the chocolate and the butter. Place the bowl over the boiling water and let it all melt together. While that's on the go, beat the whole eggs with the sugar. Use an electric whisk if you've got one, otherwise your arm's going to get quite tired. When it's getting fluffy, add the vanilla and sift in the flour. Fold the flour in and wait for the chocolate mix. When there are no lumps left in the chocolate and butter, take the bowl off the water and let the mixture cool down before adding it to the egg mixture. When the two are combined well together, pour this mix into the tray and pop it in the oven to bake for around 20 to 25 minutes. We always take ours out of the oven when it looks a bit soft in the middle still, so we get a really fudgy and gooey brownie at the end. Let them cool and cut them up into chunks. Polly really likes them with hot chocolate – you could make a mug of hot chocolate and squirt some of the cream on top, then add some marshmallows or sugar strands. This is the most yummy hot choc. Have you ever tried adding a tiny bit of chilli to hot chocolate? It's amazing.

Ingredients

375g of unsalted butter
375g dark chocolate
6 large eggs
1 tablespoon of vanilla essence
500g of caster sugar
225g of plain flour
1 teaspoon of salt
1 tray to bake them in about 20x30cm
silicone paper to line it with

How many do you think we ate!?

There are lots of things in the cocoa bean that stop you feeling blue and depressed. So eat more chocolate!

We've made a nut-free brownie but you could add nuts, raisins, chocolate chips or glacé fruits.

November
Facts & Legends

St Catherine

St Catherine was a strong and pious woman. When she was captured for her beliefs, which were different from those of the ruler of the time, she was tied to a spiked wheel and broken.

She was martyred for her beliefs and her symbol is now a wheel.
The "Catherine wheel" firework has been named after her.

Samhain, 1st Nov.

The Celts divided their year into 2 seasons, the light and the dark. In the country year Samhain marked the first day of winter, and herders brought their livestock from grazing pastures down to stables for shelter and protection. All harvest was meant to be gathered up by this time. They believed that come November the fairies would blast away every growing plant with their breath. Christians changed the day to All Saints' Day.

Armistice Day

commemorates all the men and women who lost their lives in World War I. Known also as Remembrance Day, on the 11th hour of the 11th day of the 11th month we stand in silence for 2 minutes to mark our respect.

The Lord Mayor's Show

There has been a Lord Mayor of London ever since 1189. In 1215 King John wrote a charter saying London could choose its own Lord Mayor. The King must meet the Mayor for approval and swear his loyalty.

Wind Monath

The Anglo-Saxons called November "wind monath" because it was a time when the cold winds began to blow. They also called it "blod monath", because it was the time when cattle were slaughtered for winter food.

Thanksgiving

Every 4th Thursday of November, America celebrates "Thanksgiving". It is to thank the pilgrim fathers who carved a life for them on America's boutiful land. It is also known as Black Friday or Turkey Day

Rolling of the Tar Barrels

Every year on the 5th of November, flaming tar barrels are rolled through the streets of Ottery St Mary. It starts with the smallest barrels in the morning and ends up with a giant barrel at midnight. It is a great honour to be allowed to take part. At the end of the barrel rolling festival, there is a huge bonfire that is lit with a model of Guy Fawkes on the top. It is possibly linked with burning witches.

Guy Fawkes Night

The day was called a holiday after Parliament was saved from being blown up by Guy Fawkes and his gang. They came up with the gunpowder plot in 1605. Until 1859 parish churches held services on this day. For the last 400 years, an effigy Guy Fawkes is burned on top of bonfires and fireworks are let off. Guy Fawkes is probably the most famous terrorist.

Turning the Devil's Boulder

Nobody can be sure of the dates or even year this took place, but after nightfall, men carrying crowbars and women lighting their way come close to the big stone near the church in Shebbear, Devon. As the church bells ring, the villagers try to turn over the boulder. It is said the devil lives underneath the stone, and turning it over is meant to avoid bad luck.

One legend says the stone was quarried the other side of a river near another village, and was meant to be a foundation stone for the church there, but the devil rolled it away to Shebbear, and even though the villagers rolled it back every day, it was rolled away again the next night. Maybe the stone was brought there for ritualistic reasons as it's not a type of stone found locally.

December

Jack Frost

Look out! Look out!
Jack Frost is about!
He's after our fingers and toes;
And all through the night,
The gay little sprite
Is working where nobody knows.

He'll climb each tree,
So nimble is he,
His silvery powder he'll shake.
To windows he'll creep
And while we're asleep
Such wonderful pictures he'll make.

Across the grass
He'll merrily pass,
And change all its greenness to white.
Then home he will go
And laugh ho, ho ho!
What fun I have had in the night.

by C.E. Pike

12th month

December's flower is the Narcissus

December's gemstone is the Turquoise

December originally meant the tenth month, shown here is Uller, the god of winter

MON	TUES	WED	THURS	FRI	SAT	SUN
✂ 1st Day of Advent World Aids Day **1**	**2**	**3**	International Volunteer Day St Nicholas' Eve Walt Disney. Born 1901 **4**	📖 St Nicholas' Day Enthroning of boy bishops **6**		**7**
Bodhi Day (Buddhist) Immaculate Conception (Christian) **8**	Eid al Adha (Islam) **9**	Human Rights Day **10**	**11**	Feast Day our lady of Guadalupe (Catholic Christian) **12**	St Lucia's Day Francis Drake set sail around the world in the Golden Hind 1577 **13**	**14**
15	Jane Austen, novelist. Born 1775 **16**	Wilbur and Orville Wright made the 1st powered aeroplane flight 1903 **17**	**18**	**19**	**20**	Winter solstice shortest day of the year Yule (Christian) **21**
✂ Hanukkah begins at sundown (Jewish) **22**	**23**	Christmas Eve **24**	**Christmas Day** Isaac Newton, mathematician and physicist. Born 1642 **25**	**Boxing Day** St Stephen's Day **26**	**27**	Holy Innocents Day **28**
Muharran 1st Day of New Year (Islam) **29**	Rudyard Kipling, author. Born 1865 **30**	📖 New Year's Eve Hogmanay (Scotland) **31**				

Hi Jago

I hope you are not too cold — we had a mission today to go outside and smash some holes in the ice on top of the pond so our fish can get enough air to breathe must be really tough living outside all winter! I had a jumper and a coat on and was still cold.

lots of love Polly XX

Jago Harris

204 Latimer Road

London W10 6QY

Hi Polly

We are going to London at the week-end mum is going to go Christmas shopping while dad is taking us to see the golden hind sir francis drake's galleon. Apparently there is loads of piracy stuff to do which sounds amazing will send you another postcard from it have a great holidays.

BIG KISS Jago

Polly Loughney

Honeysuckle Cottage

Lower Baldridge
Oxon OX8 4PT

Hanukkah Menorah

1 Begin by making the stand to the candlestick. Make the base quite heavy so it can take the weight of the rest of the clay you will use. If you roll the stand between your hands you can get it to about 3cm in diameter. Chop off each end to make it straight and stick it on top of the base you have made. Use a little more clay to act like glue and make it stick together.

2 The next stage is to roll 4 lengths of clay out and make them all slightly shorter than the last. Push your finger into the end of each tube to make a hole for the candle to sit in eventually. Curve the clay lengths and leave them just to go firm for about half and hour.

3 Meanwhile, roll out 3 large balls of clay and squash them slightly at either side with your finger, making a sort of ridge for the candle holders to sit on. When you have all of these pieces ready, start to assemble the Menorah.

4 Take the stand and add a little more clay to the top. Then take the longest of the curved clay candle holders and stick it to the stand, then take a ridged ball of clay and rest it on top, using a little more clay again.

5 Repeat this until the shortest curve is added to the top of the candlestick and just make sure there are no ugly bits of clay that have been squished out of the sides. If there are, use your finger to smooth them away.

6 Leave your Menorah to dry out for a few days and then you are ready to decorate it. We used spray paint, which went into every crease and crevice, but you can use a brush and paint it. While the paint is still wet, add the glitter so it sticks and leave it to dry. Then add the candles and get ready to light them for Hanukkah.

Other Ideas

Why don't you try?

*

Decorating this in lots of other pretty ways?

*

Beads

*

Rope

*

Brightly coloured paints

You will need

Modelling clay, gold paint, 8 candles, gold glitter.

Family Fish Pie

What to do

In a saucepan, melt the butter, add the flour and stir it well together. Add the milk in 2 stages. Stir well all the time to avoid lumps in your sauce. Then add the other half of the milk and stir until it begins to bubble a little at the edge of the pan. Next cut the fish into fork-sized pieces, add it to the sauce with a little salt and pepper and add some of the chopped herbs. Tip this into your pie dish. Roll-out the pastry to a bit bigger than the size of the dish. Cut a bit off each of the edges, that's about 1cm wide, and stick it with water to the edge of the dish. Next brush that ridge of pastry with water and lift the big piece of pastry on top. Push the edges together with your fingers and then cut off the extra pastry using the dish to guide your knife. With the trimmings of pastry make some decorations for the top of your pie. How about some pastry fishes and crabs? Bake the pie in quite a hot oven. Gas mark 6 or 220°C for about 25 minutes.

Ingredients

30g of butter
30g of plain flour
300ml of warmed milk
salt and pepper
400g of your favourite fish (we have used
coley, smoked haddock, dab and prawns)
1 onion
2 cloves of garlic
herbs, dill or parsley
1 packet of puff pastry

Yummy – Daddy's fish pie

Oily fish could make you clever – it contains lots of omega 3 and other brainy essential oils.

You could try using mashed or sliced potatoes if you fancy instead of pastry.

Advent Calendar

You will need

Insides of loo rolls or cling film rolls (cardboard tubes), tissue paper, glue, sticky tape, 1 dark pen, glitter, scissors, cardboard, treats that are small.

Begin by cutting 24 pieces of cardboard tube the same size. We made ours about 4 cm long. Cover one end with green tissue paper and then either glue it or tape it to the card tube.

When you have covered 1 to 24, position them into the shape of a Christmas tree and stick all of them together. We used glue but you could use tape too. When it's dried, turn it over and fill each little tube with the tiny treats. Put a different one in each tube.

Next cut a piece of card a tiny bit smaller than the shape of the tree and cover it with glue. Push this gently on to the back of the tree and leave it to dry. Don't turn it over until it's dry otherwise the treats will stick to it too.

You can hang the tree up using a picture hook or map pin and making a hole in the back of the cardboard. Next cut out the shape of the tree trunk and the bucket it's sitting in and stick it to the back of the tree, and now get ready to decorate it.

Start by writing the numbers 1 to 24 randomly on the front of the tubes and then decorate the tree. We used glitter and little pieces of scrunched-up tissue paper to look a bit like baubles.

You could use a bit of tinsel and real baubles if you like. One of Jago's friends put fairy lights around the edge of his, and it looked really pretty. The calendar is ready to use now. So when it's the first of December, push your finger through the green tissue and find the treat inside.

Cookie Wreath

Ingredients

400g of unsalted butter, 400g of caster sugar, 2 lightly beaten eggs, 800g plain flour and 25g extra for rolling out, vanilla essence, 1 baking sheet, silicone paper.

What to do

Use a bowl or an electric mixer, put in the butter and sugar and cream them together. When it's smooth, beat in the eggs and then flour, but don't mix it too much or it will spread when you bake them. Wrap the dough in cling film and then leave it to relax in the fridge for about an hour. Then, place the dough on a surface and dust it with flour. Roll it out to about 1/2cm thick and then push in your cutters to make snowflakes. Paper the baking sheet and then start to lay the cookie shapes out, overlapping them, to make a wreath shape. It's a good idea to brush them with beaten egg if you want to hang the wreath up, because it bakes even firmer. Pop your finished wreath into the oven and bake it at gas 4 or 180 °C for 25 minutes. If the cookies are still a bit transparent in places give it longer. Take out the tray and leave it to cool down completely. You can begin to decorate it. We used edible glitter and tiny sugar silver balls and lovely big bow at the bottom.

Try to think of some other shape ideas you could use. These make a gorgeous table decoration for a Hanukkah or Christmas meal. Some other shapes we like are holly leaves or stars.

Sweet Lemon Meringue Kisses

What to do

Put the egg whites into a bowl with the salt and whisk them until they hold stiff peaks. Gradually add the sugar, whisking it in all the time. When it's all mixed in, sprinkle the cornflour over the top and add the vanilla and vinegar. Beat this in too.

When you have a bowl of glistening meringue mixture, begin to splodge it on to a baking sheet covered in baking parchment. Bake each tray of meringues on gas mark 2 or 150°C for about 40 minutes or until you can peel each meringue from the paper. Spread on some of the lemon curd and then gum 2 meringues together, flat side to flat side, using the lemon cream mix. There are other kisses you can make. Use jam or chocolate if you like.

Happy kissing!

Ingredients

8 large egg whites
pinch of salt
500g caster sugar
4 teaspoons cornflour
1 teaspoon of vanilla essence
2 teaspoons of white wine vinegar
lemon curd
2 baking sheets
silicone paper

Fabulous sticky meringue treats
at our party

You could try a swirl of cocoa or a splash of rose water in your meringues.

The spanish football team real madrid is nicknamed el equipo merengue ("the meringue team" in spanish) after their white uniforms.

Father Christmas

What do you know about Father Christmas? He lives at the North Pole and has many reindeer to pull his sleigh, which he packs up with presents for all the good children in the world.

Then he flies around as quick as he can, eating mincepies in every home and then goes home to start work for the next year. He is always very happy and kind and likes to get letters from children asking him for their favourite things.

Winter Solstice

The pagan celebration of Winter Solstice is also known as Yule. It's one of the oldest winter celebrations in the world and marks the passing of the shortest day of the year and the longest night.

The druids would cut down mistletoe from oak trees and give it as a blessing. Oaks were seen as sacred and the winter fruit, mistletoe, a symbol of life. The Celts would light the Yule log to beat the darkness, banish evil spirits and to bring luck.

Advent starts at the beginning of December. It means "coming", and is associated with the Christian faith. It could be the coming of Jesus because Mary was heavily pregnant or the coming of the three wise men to see Jesus.

The Channel Tunnel was completed on 1st of December 1990. For the first time since the ice age, Britain was connected to the European mainland when workers from England and France met 40 metres under the seabed.

Mink, ermine, foxes and beavers grow beautiful coats of hair to keep them warm through winter. Some animals hibernate, some creatures, like birds and squirrels, humans help by making areas to feed them.

The Festival of Saturnalia, was a Roman 7 day feast in honour of the God of agriculture. It was a holiday when masters served their slaves, presents were given, and gambling games were played.

The Feast of St Nicholas

The patron saint of children. He used to give gifts late at night so nobody knew who it was giving. He was a rich Christian priest who then became a bishop. A famous tale about St Nicholas is about a poor man who had no money to give to his daughters on their wedding day. Saint Nicholas dropped a bag of gold into the toes of the stockings, the girls had left by the fire to dry. Maybe this is where the hanging of stockings comes from at Christmas time. Even though he was young, he had a reputation for kindness and wisdom. The Roman emperor in 303 demanded he be worshipped as a god.

The Allendale Fire Ceremony

Celebrated on the 31st of December to mark the end of the old year and the start of the new, it still goes on in parts of England. It is thought to come from pagan origins. The Allendale fire ceremony is perhaps one of the most amazing ones, with people carrying big tubs of flaming tar over their heads.

The procession eventually arrives at the town square and the flaming tubs are thrown into a bonfire. At the stroke of midnight the church bells ring out to symbolise the change from paganism to Christianity.

Index